A Visitor's Guide

The First Day of the Somme

Gommecourt to Maricourt

The Basilique Notre Dame de Brebières in Albert.

A VISITOR'S GUIDE

THE FIRST DAY OF THE SOMME

Gommecourt to Maricourt

Jon Cooksey
& Jerry Murland

Pen & Sword
MILITARY

First published in Great Britain in 2016 by
Pen & Sword Military
an imprint of
Pen & Sword Books Ltd
47 Church Street
Barnsley
South Yorkshire
S70 2AS

Copyright © Jon Cooksey and Jerry Murland, 2016

ISBN 978 1 47383 803 1

The right of Jon Cooksey and Jerry Murland to be identified as the
Authors of this Work has been asserted by them in accordance
with the Copyright, Designs and Patents Act 1988.

Typeset in Ehrhardt by
Mac Style Ltd, Bridlington, East Yorkshire
Printed and bound in the UK by CPI Group (UK) Ltd,
Croydon, CRO 4YY

Pen & Sword Books Ltd incorporates the imprints of Pen & Sword
Archaeology, Atlas, Aviation, Battleground, Discovery, Family
History, History, Maritime, Military, Naval, Politics, Railways,
Select, Transport, True Crime, and Fiction, Frontline Books, Leo
Cooper, Praetorian Press, Seaforth Publishing and Wharncliffe.

For a complete list of Pen & Sword titles please contact
PEN & SWORD BOOKS LIMITED
47 Church Street, Barnsley, South Yorkshire, S70 2AS, England
E-mail: enquiries@pen-and-sword.co.uk
Website: www.pen-and-sword.co.uk

CONTENTS

INTRODUCTION AND ACKNOWLEDGEMENTS

This guidebook focuses specifically on 1 July 1916 – the opening day of what has become known as the Battle of the Somme, a campaign that lasted for almost five months. Each of the eleven routes we have chosen between Gommecourt in the north and Montauban in the south provides the battlefield visitor with the opportunity to walk or bike the ground that was fought over on that fateful first day. Linking each route is a 'spine route' which can be either cycled or driven and, as far as is possible, follows the British front line. By completing each of the eleven routes and following the connecting 'spine', the battlefield tourist is able to cover the whole of the British sector from Gommecourt to Maricourt.

We have continued to design routes that give the battlefield tourist the opportunity to appreciate and explore the more remote parts of the front line. The French region of Picardy is blessed with a varied landscape of wooded, rolling hills and shallow valleys and on clear days the views from the high ground can be quite invigorating. In addition we have included visits to 130 sites and memorials and 48 British, French and German cemeteries. Where possible we have used quiet roads and local pathways but please do be aware that speeding traffic and farm machinery is always a possibility even on the quietest of roads.

Whilst we have ensured vehicles are not left in isolated spots we do recommend you take the usual precautions when leaving a vehicle unattended by placing valuables securely in the boot or out of sight. The guidebook highlights what the battlefields look like today and consequently you will find few contemporary photographs, but, like the battlefields of 1916, the weather remains unpredictable. We have been blessed with fine weather on our frequent visits to the area but it is always advisable to carry a set of waterproofs and have a sensible pair of boots or shoes to walk in. Cafes and refreshment stops are few and far between and although we have mentioned those places where refreshments are served, it is prudent to take something to eat and drink when away from your vehicle. Cyclists will recognize the need to use a set of multi-terrain tyres on their bikes and perhaps a sturdier off-road machine as a number of the tracks we use can become muddy after periods of rain.

The historical information provided with each route has, of necessity, been limited by space but we have given an overview around which to develop your understanding of what took place and why. Nevertheless, we have made some additional suggestions for further reading which should widen your appreciation of the events that took place on this sector of the Western Front 100 years ago. Visitors to the Fricourt German Cemetery will appreciate the section covering equivalent ranks and those of you who wish to find the last resting place of the soldier poets or the Victoria Cross winners will find the appendices of use.

In acknowledging the assistance of others we must thank James Buchanan from the *Rutland Remembers* website for permission to use the photograph of the Thiepval Memorial and ww1battlefields.co.uk for permission to use the photograph of the Manchesters Memorial at Mametz. Sebastian Laudan in Germany has once again gone out of his way with his assistance on German queries, whilst Alan MacDonald, author of *A Lack of Offensive Spirit? – The 46th (North Midland) Division at Gommecourt, 1st July 1916* and *Pro Patria Mori: The 56th (1st London) Division at Gommecourt, 1st July 1916*, kindly read drafts of the sections on the fighting at Gommecourt and made helpful suggestions. Thanks also to Michael Stedman, who offered his knowledgeable insights into the fighting south of la Boisselle, Jeremy Banning and Richard van Emden who kindly nudged us towards sources for the right flank actions around Montauban and Maricourt, and to Dr Michelle Macleod, Senior Lecturer in Gaelic at the University of Aberdeen, for her help in translating the inscriptions on the Highlanders' memorials.

VISITING MILITARY CEMETERIES

The concept of the **Imperial War Graves Commission** (IWGC) was created by **Major Fabian Ware** (1869–1949), the volunteer leader of a Red Cross mobile unit which saw service on the Western Front for most of the period of the war. Concern for the identification and burial of the dead led him to begin lobbying for an organization devoted to the burial and maintenance of the graves of those who had been killed or died in the service of their country. On 21 May 1917 the Prince of Wales became the president of the IWGC with **Fabian Ware** as its vice-chairman. Forty-three years later the IWGC became the **Commonwealth War Graves Commission (CWGC)**. Neither a soldier nor a politician, Ware was later honoured

The concept of what became the CWGC was first created by Fabian Ware in 1917.

with a knighthood and held the honorary rank of major general. The commission was responsible for introducing the standardized headstone which ensured equality in death regardless of rank, race or creed and it is this familiar white headstone that you will see now in CWGC cemeteries all over the world. In the area covered by this guidebook we have referred to and described forty-three cemeteries containing British and Commonwealth casualties. CWGC cemeteries are usually well signposted with the familiar green and white direction indicators and where there is a CWGC plot within a communal cemetery, such as **Auchonvillers Communal Cemetery**, the green and white sign at the entrance, with the words *Tombes de Guerre du Commonwealth*, will indicate their presence. The tall Cross of Sacrifice with the bronze Crusader's sword can be found in many

CWGC Cemeteries are marked with the familiar green and white sign boards.

CWGC plots within a communal cemetery are marked with a green and white sign containing the words *Tombes de Guerre du Commonwealth* at the entrance.

The pattern of Corporal Bill Sweatman's headstone (IX.F.7) at Dantzig Alley Cemetery is of a standard pattern – the 'World War' pattern which you will find across all First and Second World War CWGC cemeteries. Post-war CWGC headstones have a notch cut into either shoulder at the top.

cemeteries, such as **Dantzig Alley British Cemetery**, where there are relatively large numbers of dead. The larger cemeteries, **Serre Road Cemetery No. 2** for example, also have the rectangular shaped Stone of Remembrance. A visitor's book and register of casualties is usually kept in a bronze box by the entrance. Sadly, a number of registers have been stolen and to prevent this from happening you may find a cemetery register is now kept in the local *Mairie*.

CWGC cemeteries are noted for their high standards of horticultural excellence and the image of rows of headstones set amidst grass pathways and flowering shrubs is one every battlefield visitor takes away with them. On each headstone is the badge of the regiment or corps, or in the case of Commonwealth forces, the national emblem. Below that is the name and rank of the individual and the date on which they died together with any decoration they may have received. Headstones of Victoria Cross winners, such as that of **Sergeant James Turnbull** in the **Lonsdale Cemetery** at Authille, have the additional motif of the decoration on their headstone. At the base of the headstone is often an inscription which has been chosen by the family. Headstones marking the unidentified bear the inscriptions chosen by Rudyard Kipling, 'A Soldier of the Great War' or, 'Known Unto God'. Special memorials are erected to casualties known to be buried in a particular cemetery but whose precise location is uncertain.

French War Graves

There are two French National Cemeteries in the area covered by this guidebook, the *Cimetière National de Serre-Hébuterne* and the *Cimetière*

National de Albert on the D938 southeast of the town, but the visitor will find the white concrete grave markers used by the French *Ministère de la Défense et des Anciens Combattants* in a number of CWGC cemeteries and plots. Typical of these are the headstones of **Georges Palvadeau** and **Louis Lesourd** at Railway Hollow Cemetery near Serre.

German Cemeteries

The German War Graves Commission – *Volksbund Deutsche Kriegs-gräberfürsorge* – is responsible for the maintenance and upkeep of German war graves in Europe and North Africa. As with CWGC cemeteries, these are clearly signposted with a black and white sign bearing the words *Deutscher Soldatenfriedhof*. The German cemeteries are in stark contrast to the CWGC cemeteries in that they frequently exude a dark and often sombre ambiance exacerbated by the black grave markers bearing the name, rank, date of death and occasionally the unit. Like many French cemeteries, they often contain mass graves for the unidentified and headstones can carry up to three or four names on each one. We would recommend you visit the German cemetery at **Fricourt**, which can provide the battlefield tourist with a greater understanding of the huge loss of life that occurred on both sides of the conflict.

German cemeteries are signposted with a black and white sign bearing the words Deutscher Soldatenfriedhof.

Equivalent Ranks

When visiting German military cemeteries it can be confusing when trying to understand the various ranks of the soldiers buried there. There is only one German cemetery in the sector covered by this guidebook but you will find German headstones in CWGC cemeteries. We have produced a rough guide to equivalent ranks which should assist you when visiting the cemeteries and memorials referred to.

British	German
British	**German**
Field Marshal	*Generalfeldmarschall*
General	*Generaloberst*
Lieutenant General	*General der Infantrie/Artillerie/Kavallerie*
Major General	*Generalmajor*
Brigadier General	No equivalent rank
Colonel	*Oberst*
Lieutenant Colonel	*Oberstleutnant*
Major	*Major*
Captain	*Hauptmann/Rittmeister*
Lieutenant	*Oberleutnant*
Second Lieutenant	*Leutnant*
Warrant Officer	*Feldwebelleutnant*
Sergeant Major	*Offizierstellvertreter*
Sergeant	*Vize-Feldwebel*
Corporal	*Unteroffizer/Oberjäger*
Lance Corporal	*Gefreiter/Obergefreiter*
Private	*Schütze/Grenadier/Jäger/Musketier/Soldat/ Pionier/Fahrer/Füsilier Kanonier*

HISTORICAL CONTEXT

The Battle of the Somme opened with what is still recognized as the British Army's bloodiest day on Saturday, 1 July 1916 and concluded nearly five months later on 18 November with the fighting on the heights above the River Ancre. British casualties on the first day alone were 57,470 of which 19,240 were killed, a figure that touched almost every town and village in Britain. The relentless German pressure on, and correspondingly huge French losses at, Verdun since 21 February 1916 not only reduced their contribution of men and materiel to the offensive on the Somme but also increased the urgency for the British to launch the attack. With the principal role in the campaign now devolved to the British under the overall command of **General Sir Douglas Haig**, the British defined their objectives as reducing the pressure on the French at Verdun, assisting their allies in the East and the infliction of losses on the Germans with exploitation if the initial attack was successful. The French Sixth Army, under the command of **General Émile Fayolle**, with one corps on the north bank from Maricourt to the Somme and two corps on the south bank southwards to Foucaucourt, would make a subsidiary attack to guard the right flank of the main British attack.

General Sir Douglas Haig.

General Émile Fayolle.

Many of the British units that attacked the German line on 1 July were filled with men of Kitchener's New Army who had volunteered for service with locally raised 'Pals' battalions. These were men who had answered the call of duty early in the war and fully expected they would be part of the 'Big Push' on the Somme which would end it. Woefully short on battle experience but brimming with a naïve and infectious enthusiasm, these men were witness to the seven-day artillery bombardment that began on 24 June and sent over 3 million shells crashing onto the German forward defences during the

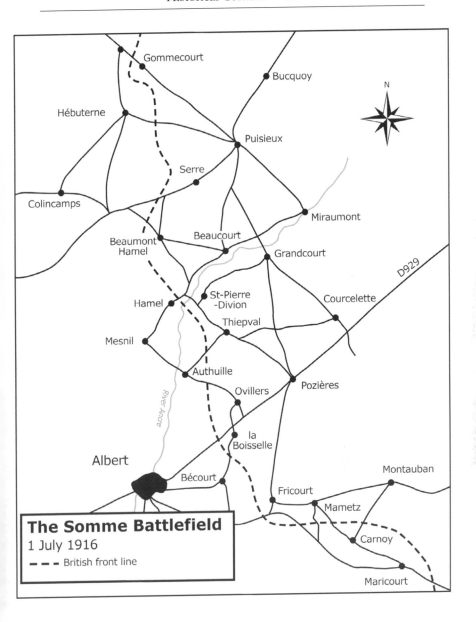

The Somme Battlefield
1 July 1916
- - - British front line

week that followed. This bombardment was designed to cut the German wire in front of the first- and second-line trenches, destroy dugouts, machine-gun and trench-mortar positions and reduce the line-holding garrisons to gibbering wrecks. Z-Day was originally planned for 29 June 1916 but bad weather postponed the assault until 1 July.

On the northernmost flank of the battleground two divisions of **Lieutenant General Sir Edmund Allenby's** Third Army were given the task of creating a diversion to draw enemy forces away from the main attack further south being spearheaded by **Lieutenant General Sir Henry Rawlinson's** Fourth Army. A second diversionary attack was made 60km to the north near Neuve Chapelle when the Royal Sussex of 116 Brigade attacked the Boar's Head Salient, an action that is covered in our guide *The Battles of French Flanders*. Rawlinson's fifteen divisions were spread along the front line that ran south of Gommecourt to Maricourt where the French Sixth Army supported the British assault with five divisions. Thus, including reserves, the total number of Allied troops involved on the first day of the assault was ¾ million men distributed amongst 27 divisions. Facing them was a well-entrenched German Second Army with less than sixteen divisions at its disposal.

Lieutenant General Sir Edmund Allenby.

At the conclusion of the first day the only successes along the 18-mile-long battle front were to the south of the D929 Albert–Bapaume road where the British – securing all their objectives – captured Montauban and Mametz and the French Sixth Army made considerable progress towards Péronne. In stark contrast – and roughly north of the

Lieutenant General Sir Henry Rawlinson.

road – many proud British battalions were scythed down in minutes as they crossed no-man's-land or struggled through thickets of uncut wire pursued by German defenders who rose from deep dugouts unmolested by the British artillery. Apart from tiny toeholds in the Leipzig Salient above Authille and the front line northwest of Thiepval, the British were forced back to their start lines. German casualties are difficult to estimate with absolute accuracy due to their meaning of casualties and accounting periods, but on the British sector losses were estimated to be a little over about 8,000 men, amongst them more than 2,000 prisoners and 4,500 wounded. Around 1,500 men were killed, a ratio of German to British dead of about 1:15! The successes at Montauban and Mametz were little mitigation for an almost overwhelming disaster.

The impact of the Somme – especially the cataclysmic first day – has become rooted deep in the psyche of the British population over the last 100 years, mainly through imagery – mud, more mud and misery – and first-hand testimony. Over the intervening years this coloured people's perceptions and led to an extremely emotive and narrow view of the First World War as a whole. Ask the average individual today to list the major battles that took place between 1914 and 1918 and the Somme will probably top the list along with Passchendaele (the Third Battle of Ypres), which we cover in our *Ypres* guidebook. Rather unfairly, Haig and Rawlinson have been the subject of criticism ever since, critics pointing particularly to the futility of the attacks, the 'waste' of lives and the failure to achieve territorial objectives. Criticism of Haig, particularly with regard to the almost incomprehensible numbers of casualties sustained and his continuance of the offensive when all original objectives had evaporated, has obscured his later achievements under a cloud of perceived callousness and indifference. It is a view felt by many historians to be unfair and inaccurate. Today, a growing number agree that there was no strategic alternative for the British in 1916 and that the horror generated by the extensive casualty lists is an insular one, given the millions of casualties already suffered by the French and Russian armies since the outbreak of war in 1914. Others continue to lay blame at the door of the commanding generals to whom Haig had subordinated the details of the planning and refuse to accept that the Somme battlefields of 1916 were the bloody classrooms of a 'hard school' in which the men of Kitchener's New Army learned some very 'hard lessons' very quickly and won their spurs in the first industrial war, a war in which the mass continental armies of other nations had been engaged for two years. And on that first day, of course, there was little to cheer. The learning came at a terrible price.

Perhaps we should turn to the words of historian Martin Middlebrook who, in his seminal *The First Day on the Somme* (1971), wrote: 'The only good to emerge from that terrible day was the display of patriotism, courage and self-sacrifice shown by the British soldiers. Theirs is a memory that their country should always cherish.'

VISITING THE AREA

Visitors to the Somme can either stay in one of the larger urban centres such as Albert and Amiens or avail themselves of the myriad of bed and breakfast and self-catering establishments available. In Albert the **Royal Picardie Hotel** is good, as is the **Hotel de la Paix** and for occasional meals the authors can recommend the **Cafe Hygge** opposite the Basilique Notre Dame de Brebières. Alternatively, 33km to the southwest the cathedral city of Amiens offers the more luxurious **Hotel Marotte** and the **Mercure Amiens Cathédrale**. However, there is a wide choice of self-catering and bed and breakfast accommodation around the battlefield which places you 'on site' amongst the rolling hills of Picardy. A search online will reveal many of these but we can recommend both **Chavasse Farm** – which has three self-catering cottages – and **Les Alouettes** – http://lesalouettes.net/ – in Hardecourt aux Bois. **Snowden House** in Longueval – see also www.chavasseferme. co.uk or phone Jonathan Porter on +0044 (0)7855850889 – sleeps up to sixteen guests in five bedrooms. A very comfortable self-catering cottage

Albert has a number of hotels and restaurants.

The Ocean Villa Tea Rooms at Auchonvillers is owned and run by Avril Williams.

in Morval is **Maison Lavande** – http://www.lochnagar.fr/user_contact.php – owned and run by Julia and Bob Paterson, phone +0044 (0)1382 775000 or +0044 (0)7962 423156.

In Auchonvillers **Beaumont Hamel View** – +0033 (0) 965 235 563 – has four en-suite bedrooms and provides a good breakfast as well as having secure storage for bikes and drying facilities, whereas **Avril Williams' Ocean Villa Guest House & Tea Rooms** nearby has seven bedrooms, an adjoining cafe and is on the site of a former dressing station – www.avrilwilliams.eu.

Campers will find **Camping Bellevue** at Authuille open from March to October each year and situated in a delightful location close to the battlefields. The site benefits from a nearby restaurant and has static caravans to rent and facilities for motor homes. **Camping le Véledrome** in Albert is in a more central location and also has facilities for camper vans and mobile homes for rent. In all cases we recommend you book early to avoid disappointment.

It goes without saying that walkers and cyclists should be properly equipped to enjoy their activity. The weather is often unpredictable and it is always advisable to walk in a decent pair of boots and carry a set of waterproofs with you. Regular visitors to the battlefields will be familiar with the collections of old shells and other explosive material that is often placed by the roadside by farmers. By all means look but please do not touch as much of it is still in an unstable condition.

Using this Guidebook

The Somme area is characterized by its rolling hills and valleys and whilst walkers should have little difficulty, bikers will need a decent off-road machine equipped with suitable tyres as some of the tracks we describe can become slippery after rain. In compiling the guide we have taken the liberty of using a number of abbreviations in the text. With German units we have simply trimmed Infanterie Regiment and Reserve Infanterie Regiment to IR and RIR. Thus, Infanterie Regiment No. 157 becomes IR 157 and Reserve Infanterie Regiment No. 165 becomes RIR 165. British battalions and units have also been abbreviated, for example the 10th Battalion West Yorkshire Regiment becoming 10/West Yorks.

Unexploded ammunition is a common sight on the former battlefields. Look by all means but do not touch.

As this volume focuses on 1 July 1916 we have added the approximate positions of the German and British front lines to each route map to give the battlefield tourist an idea of where the respective lines were. Where we refer to casualties the number quoted is usually taken from the battalion's war diary and includes officers and men who were killed, wounded, missing or taken prisoner after the engagement.

We have not drawn specific maps for the spine routes and although our route maps do touch on these sectors, the spine routes are best supported by the French Institut Géographique National (IGN) 1:100,000 maps which can be purchased at most good tourist offices and online from www.mapsworldwide.com. However, we do recommend satellite navigation in supporting general route finding. For the walker and cyclist, the larger scale French 1:25,000 Série Bleue maps which cover the area (2407O – Acheux-en-Amiénois; 2407E – Bapaume; 2408O – Albert; and 2408E – Bray-sur-Somme) can be bought in France or online and can be downloaded onto your tablet.

The relevant map should be used when out walking or cycling to supplement the basic maps provided in the guide. To assist in your route choice we have provided a summary of all eleven routes in the guidebook together with an indication as to their suitability for walkers, cyclists or car tourists. Distances are in km – the first figure in the table – and miles. You will find that the circular alphanumeric references in the text of each route correspond directly with those on the relevant map.

Route No.	Route	Distance	🚶	🚲	🚗
1	Gommecourt North	4.7km/2.9 miles	✔		
2	Gommecourt South	5.8km/3.6 miles	✔	✔	
	Spine Route – Gommecourt to Serre	8.6km/5.3 miles		✔	✔
3	Serre	5.2km/3.2 miles	✔	✔	
4	Serre – alternative start	3.7km/2.3 miles	✔	✔	
	Spine Route – Serre Road Cemetery No. 1 to Beaumont Hamel	2.6km/1.6 miles		✔	✔
5	Beaumont Hamel	6.5km/4.0 miles	✔	✔	
	Spine Route – Beaumont Hamel to Ulster Tower	6.6km/4.1 miles		✔	✔
6	Thiepval Spur	7.9km/4.9 miles	✔	✔	
	Spine Route – Ulster Tower to Ovillers-la-Boisselle	5.5km/3.4 miles		✔	✔
7	Ovillers-la-Boisselle	7.2km/4.5 miles	✔	✔	
	Spine Route – Ovillers-la-Boisselle to la Boisselle	2.6km/1.6 miles		✔	✔
8	la Boisselle	6.8km/4.2 miles	✔	✔	
	Spine Route – la Boisselle to Fricourt	7.4km/4.6 miles		✔	✔
9	Fricourt	7.2km/4.8 miles	✔	✔	
	Spine Route – Fricourt to Mametz	2.4km/1.5 miles		✔	✔
10	Mametz	4.0km/2.5 miles	✔	✔	
	Spine Route – Mametz to Montauban	3.3km/2.1 miles		✔	✔
11	Montauban	7.9km/4.9 miles	✔	✔	
	Spine Route – Montauban to Maricourt	3.2km/1.9 miles		✔	✔

British Battalions on the Somme

Soon after the outbreak of war in 1914 each Territorial Force (TF) battalion was required to form a reserve battalion to provide it with reinforcements. Thus, in addition to the regular battalions, when enough men of, for example, the 5th (TF) Battalion of the York and Lancaster Regiment (5/York and Lancs) had volunteered to serve overseas – Imperial Service – it became the 'first-line' battalion with a 'second-line' battalion at home. The 'first' and 'second-line' battalions were re-titled in early 1915 so that 5/York and Lancs became 1/5 with the second-line battalion becoming the 2/5 based in England on home service or providing the necessary reinforcements. In March 1915 all TF units were required to form a third reserve battalion leaving the first- and second-line battalions to become operational and the third battalion – the 3/5 – to train and supply reinforcements. **Service battalions** were raised as part of Lord Kitchener's 'New Army' of volunteers as additional battalions of a regiment and were distinguished by the word 'Service' as in the 6th (Service) Battalion. Thus, the York and Lancaster Regiment produced eight service battalions in addition to six TF battalions. New Army battalions were sometimes known by their unofficial title which signified their town or city of origin. Many of these **Pals Battalions** – a phrase first coined by Lord Derby – first saw action on 1 July 1916 and

Men of the 16th Middlesex Regiment (Public Schools Battalion) at White City prior to their attack astride the New Beaumont Road towards Beaumont Hamel.

Men of the 4th Worcestershire Regiment, 29th Division, marching to the trenches, 27 June 1916.

sustained heavy casualties which impacted greatly on the communities from which they had been raised. Thus, for example, the 10th Battalion Lincolnshire Regiment was known as the Grimsby Chums and the 12th, 13th and 14th Battalions York and Lancaster Regiment went under the names of the Sheffield City Battalion and the 1st and 2nd Barnsley Pals respectively. When visiting CWGC cemeteries you may notice that the headstones of men of the Liverpool Pals battalions occasionally carry the crest of Lord Derby's eagle and child instead of their regimental badge whilst the regimental numbers of men of the Sheffield and Barnsley battalions carry the prefix 12, 13 or 14. With the introduction of conscription in 1916, the close-knit nature of the Pals Battalions was never again replicated.

Gommecourt North

A circular tour beginning at: the *Mairie*
Coordinates: 50°08'21.35" N – 2°38'43.11" E
Distance: 4.7km/2.9 miles
Suitable for: 🚶
Grade: Easy (total ascent 29m)
Maps: IGN Série Bleue 2407O – Acheux-en-Amiénois

General description and context: This route covers the 46th (North Midland) Division attack of 1 July which, along with the 56th (1st London) Division attack, was designed to direct attention away from the Fourth Army assault further south. This short route may be suitable for walkers only as the track leading up to the **'Z'** and **'Little Z'** trenches can be difficult to negotiate by bike. The route can also be combined with **Route 2** to make a longer figure-of-eight tour of the whole sector.

The inherent strength of the German position at Gommecourt was in part due to geography. The westerly projection of a wooded area called Gommecourt Park to the immediate southwest of the village formed the 'Gommecourt Salient', its western 'snout' – the most westerly of all German-held territory in France – marked by a single tree called the 'Kaiser's Oak'. This salient afforded the Germans almost complete observation and dominance of the British lines to the south and therefore good flanking fields of small arms and, more important, artillery fire towards the area of the main assault. In addition, the distance between the two opposing lines was greater than the norm: no-man's-land at its widest point in front of the 46th Division measured 400m, a factor that had not gone unnoticed by the **Hon. Major General Edward Montagu-Stuart-Wortley**, who had been in command of the division since June 1914. Although efforts to reduce this distance with the construction of a new 'assault

Major General Montagu-Stuart-Wortley.

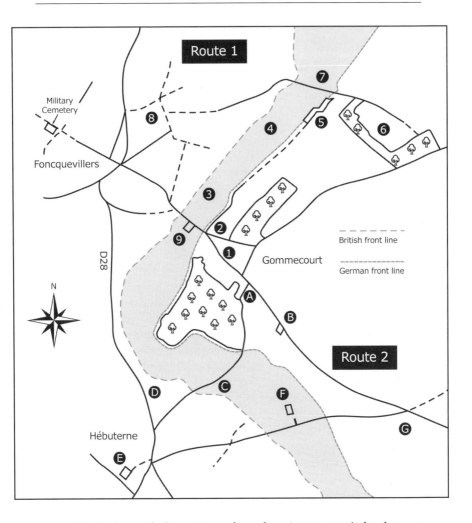

trench', 80m beyond the existing front line in no-man's-land, went some way to improving the situation, there was a considerable cost in human terms as **Private Thomas Higgins** of 1/5 North Staffordshires was to discover on the night of 23/24 June 1916 when he was part of a large covering party protecting the diggers of working parties north of the Foncquevillers–Gommecourt road:

> We heard a loud shout in German. Then Hell and its fury broke loose over us. He [the Germans] rained trench mortars on those who were digging. Shells in hundreds were dropped on our trenches. On us, the covering party, they turned dozens of machine guns.

He got our range just right. The bullets came like streams of water from hose pipes.... The terrible horror of that night is impossible to describe. My mate was riddled with bullets at the first discharge. He soon died. We lay with our faces pressed in the wet grass and wondered how many more seconds of life were left to us.

Three men were killed including, as Thomas Higgins said, his great pal, Arthur Lomas. Twenty men were wounded with one missing.

The German defences along this sector of the front hosted a profusion of deep shelters and well-developed trench lines which had been constructed over many relatively undisturbed months. Holding the German line opposite the understrength and illness-weakened 46th Division were the men of RIR 55 and RIR 91 together with artillery from the 2nd Guard Reserve Division and the 52nd Division. The eastern end of Gommecourt village was contained in a particularly strong fortification called **Kern Redoubt** by the Germans which together with the network of trenches between the southeast corner of Gommecourt Park and Gommecourt Communal Cemetery – known by the British as **The Maze –** had the added security of three heavily wired trench lines, which completely enclosed the salient before running northeast through Gommecourt Wood towards the **Z Trenches** and **Pigeon Wood**. British trench maps identified the various sectors of the German front line by allocating them names beginning with the letter F. Thus, we have 'Face' on the right flank of the 56th Division running round Gommecourt Park up to 'Food', which was opposite the sector to be attacked by 1/7 (Robin Hood Rifles), Nottinghamshire and Derbyshire Regiment – The Sherwood Foresters – on the left flank of the 46th Division. Communication trenches followed a similar system using the letter E for the 56th Division and the letter O for the 46th Division.

The 46th Division attack was carried out by **137 Brigade** on the right flank and **139 Brigade** on the left. **138 Brigade** – less two battalions – was kept in reserve. There was to be no frontal assault on Gommecourt Park or the village proper: the object was to attack north of the Gommecourt–Foncquevillers road and, by 'joining hands' beyond the village at a point called **The Quadrilateral** with the 56th Division – attacking from the southeast – 'pinch out' the Gommecourt Salient before both divisions turned to clear the village and the defences of Gommecourt Park.

On the morning of the assault 137 Brigade were only halfway across no-man's-land before the Germans opened fire, and those that reached the German wire found it to be largely uncut and this, together with the German artillery bombardment of no-man's-land, effectively destroyed

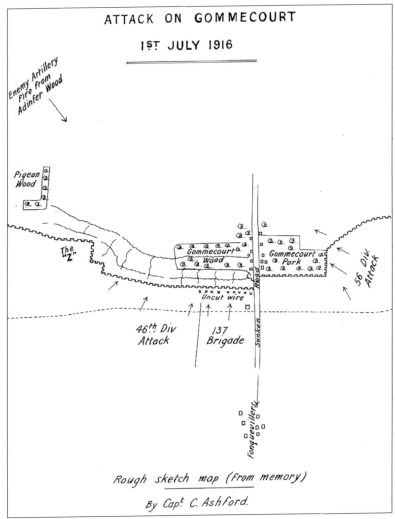

Rough sketch of the attack on Gommecourt, drawn from memory by 137 Brigade Intelligence Officer Captain Cyril Ashford.

any further aspirations of breaching the German trenches. On the left flank, 139 Brigade did achieve some success. Three waves of Sherwood Foresters broke into the German front line and some even reached the second-line defences but the German machine-gun and artillery barrage prevented further units from joining them and touch with the leading lines was lost. Attempts were made to renew the attack around the north end of Gommecourt Wood, where it was thought some Sherwood Foresters were still fighting, but the poor state of the trenches, congested with dead and wounded and discarded equipment, delayed this until 3.00pm. Then only a few men of the 1/6 Sherwood Foresters left the trenches to be shot down immediately. The last remnants of the 56th Division eventually abandoned a small stretch of German trench to the east of Gommecourt Park at about 7.30pm. The 46th Division suffered 2,455 officers and men killed, wounded or missing. Amongst the casualties were four commanding officers, **Lieutenant Colonel Dennis Wilson** of 1/5 Sherwood Foresters, **Lieutenant Colonel Lawrence Hind** of 1/7 Sherwood Foresters, **Lieutenant Colonel Charles Boote,** commanding 1/6 North Staffordshires and 36-year-old **Lieutenant Colonel William Burnett** commanding 1/5 North Staffordshires who died of his wounds on 3 July 1916. Famously, the 46th Division was accused of demonstrating 'a lack of offensive spirit'. Major General Montagu-Stuart-Wortley was stripped of his command on 5 July 1916 and replaced by Major General William Thwaites.

Directions to start: Gommecourt is situated on the D6 between Foncquevillers and Puisieux. Park outside the *Mairie*.

Route description: Gommecourt is a quiet rural village with no shops or cafes and was adopted by Wolverhampton after the war. From the *Mairie* – where there is a plaque on the wall commemorating the 1/5 North Staffordshires – walk towards the church ❶ passing the village war memorial on your left. Where the road bends and meets the Rue de Linchaux on the right is where the German front line crossed – from left to right – in front of you. Ahead on the left you will see **Gommecourt Wood New British Cemetery** which we will visit on the return leg of the walk. Our route takes the first narrow metalled track on the right heading northeast across the fields towards a long line of trees and shrubs. ❷ After 90m this road, which soon degenerates into a farm track, follows the course of the old German front line, which ran exactly along the line of the track.

Continue along the track. **Gommecourt Wood – Bois du Sartel** on modern maps – is on the right and there were two further lines of German support trenches between you and the edge of Gommecourt Wood together with a further belt of barbed wire – an altogether formidable defence line. After 150m stop and look over the fields – le Bois Batard – to your left. ❸ The approximate position of the newly dug British assembly trenches line ran roughly from the point where the electricity lines cross the road beyond the cemetery on the left

Gommecourt church and war memorial.

and followed the line of the pylons, the original line being some 80m beyond. This was the ground over which 137 Brigade attacked on 1 July, the first wave made up of men of 1/6 South Staffordshires – nearest the road – with 1/6 North Staffordshires to their left. These men were cut down by German machine-gunners as they advanced towards you.

Private Thomas Higgins was in the second attack with 1/5 North Staffordshires and remembered that the '6th North were practically wiped out when we got to them.' His battalion's attack went over the top in a long line which,'did not last for long. Men were falling over like skittles bowled over. Some would sink down in a heap, others would shout and throw their hands up and totter forward a pace or two then fall face downwards, never to rise again.'Thomas Higgins' commanding officer, **Lieutenant Colonel Burnett**, had gone missing but he was seen several hours later, lying mortally wounded in the communication trench that led to the British advanced trench.

As the track peters out follow the field edge as it passes to the left of the long line of trees and shrubs ahead of you. Across to your left ❹ would have been the ground over which the 1/5 and 1/7 Sherwood Foresters of 139 Brigade advanced. **Private Stevenson** of the 1/7 Robin Hoods recorded the moment 5 Platoon, B Company attacked: 'We go over the top. Lieutenant Wilkins leads. . . . "Come on the Robins!" Out of the smoke come bullets. Someone falls dead. On we go.'Having suffered

The Z Trenches

Pigeon Wood

Track following the approximate position of the German front line on 1 July 1916

Looking north towards the site of 'Little Z' and 'The Z' Trenches and Pigeon Wood.

enormous casualties crossing no-man's-land due to heavy enfilade fire from Little Z, some managed to get into the German front line. Imagine now, for a moment, the ground to your left – sodden from earlier heavy rain – littered with the bodies of the dead and wounded. Imagine men hanging on the uncut German wire, the earth pockmarked with shell holes into which small groups of men huddle to seek refuge whilst the few remaining officers desperately try to urge their men forward under a flailing maelstrom of small arms and shell fire. By the time the remnants – including Private Stevenson and **Second Lieutenant Alfred Wilkins** – reached the German front line, **Lieutenant Colonel Dennis Wilson** and **Lieutenant Colonel Lawrence Hind** had already been shot down and killed. Their bodies were never found. Hind is remembered on the Thiepval Memorial to the Missing but Wilson, being an Indian Army officer in the 17th Cavalry, had his name inscribed on the Indian Memorial at Neuve Chapelle. Stevenson survived but his platoon had been reduced by two-thirds. He never saw Second Lieutenant Wilkins again. Like his commanding officer, Lawrence Hind, he is remembered on the Thiepval Memorial.

Behind the assaulting waves came the 1/6 Sherwood Foresters under the command of **Lieutenant Colonel Godfrey Goodman**. Goodman's command had been designated the support and carrying battalion for 139 Brigade. As with many of the battalions in front of them, the 1/6 Sherwoods were tired even before they reached their jumping off point. **Private John Bates** of A Company recalled, 'we had three bags of bombs to carry, a pair of wire cutters, 200 rounds of bullets, a shovel or pick and we were standing in the trenches all night up to our knees in water'. Another A Company man who was advancing with the fifth wave of assaulting infantry was 20-year-old **Sergeant Richard (Dick) Wagg.** He and his platoon had only advanced some 30m into no-man's-land when he found himself the only NCO left on his feet. Carrying his wounded platoon officer – 26-year-old **Lieutenant Ronald Wheatcroft** – back to the trenches, he returned twice more to bring in wounded men. His award of the DCM was announced in September 1916. Sadly, Wheatcroft died of his wounds the next day. It was in this vicinity that **Captain John Green,** the medical officer attached to the 1/5 Sherwood Foresters, went to the assistance of 23-year-old **Captain Frank Robinson** who had been badly wounded and was ensnared on the German wire entanglements. Under heavy fire Green dragged the wounded Robinson into a nearby shell hole and dressed his wounds. Green was killed bringing him to safety: his award of the **Victoria Cross** was announced in August 1916. Unfortunately, Robinson died of his wounds two days later.

The track at this point is often indistinct but continue to follow the field's edge. Up ahead is a large clump of trees and shrubs ❺, the near edge of which is the site of **Little Z** – so named because the German front line at this point was kinked in the shape of the letter 'Z'. You will walk the line of it now. From Little Z the line ran north to describe an even larger 'Z' just prior to meeting the track you can see some 300m further on.

As you bear left towards the copse and the large electricity pylon on its left-hand edge, the expanse of the Bois des Dames – **Pigeon Wood** to British troops – comes into view across to your right. ❻

By heading towards the electricity pylon you will soon arrive at the left-hand edge of the copse where you can gain access to the former German front-line trenches that are masked by the trees. These trenches remain in remarkable condition and it is still possible to walk along the trench through the old firing bays for about 150m. Although not directly in the path of the assault of 139 Brigade, the **Little Z** trenches were briefly entered by men of C Company 1/7 Sherwood Foresters who swung to the left during their advance.

After leaving the Little Z trenches – ignoring the piles of unexploded shells – look back the way you have come and consider how machine guns in these trenches could pour flanking fire across the entire front of the 46th Division. Continue towards the pylon ahead from where you will be able to see a track to your left. Follow the field edge to the junction of tracks and stop. ❼ This is the approximate position of **The Z** where

The former German Trenches between 'Little Z' and 'The Z'.

the German front line turned 90 degrees east and ran along the line of the track towards the northwestern edge of Pigeon Wood. The German name for The Z was the *'Schwalbennest'* – swallow's nest – its shape from the air, with its lattice work of trenches, resembling the bird's nest jammed into a triangular gap in a wall, a corner or under eaves. It was a strong position which completely dominated their 'Gommecourt – Nord' sector. Enfilade fire from this protruding point also wreaked havoc amongst the assaulting troops crossing no-man's-land.

Turn left and take the left fork after 80m and stop by the pylon on the right of the track. In the distance you should be able to see Foncquevillers church and across to your left is the wooded area of Little Z which you have just visited. You are now standing on the British front line which crossed the track at this point to run parallel to the German trench line you have just followed, before heading north towards Monchy-au-Bois. On the skyline in the distance is Gommecourt Wood.

Continue along the track – known as **la Brayelle Road** or **Whizzbang Avenue** on trench maps – through the section of sunken road to reach a T-junction. Ahead of you is **Sniper's Square ❽** which hosted numerous artillery units on 1 July but was better known by the troops as 'a place to keep your head down'. Turn left and continue uphill to another junction of tracks and a calvary where you should bear left towards Gommecourt. You are now on the eastern edge of Foncquevillers – known by the troops as 'Funky Villas' – which was the forward base for the 46th Division during July 1916 and was adopted by Derby after the war. Having passed the communal cemetery on your right, you should be able to see Gommecourt church in the distance. At the next T-junction turn right along a straight narrow track to the junction with the D6. Turn left towards Gommecourt and **Gommecourt Wood New Cemetery** ❾ is 250m further along the road on the right.

The cemetery is a post-war concentration of graves which now contains 739 casualties, of which almost two-thirds are unidentified. The headstones of ten casualties known or believed to have been buried here lie either side of the Cross of Sacrifice. Situated in no-man's-land, the cemetery looks straight over the ground over which the 46th Division attacked on 1 July and a large number of the dead buried here are casualties of that assault. About 25m from the steps of the cemetery, situated in the middle of no-man's-land in 1916, were the ruins of the Gommecourt sugar refinery. Here 41-year-old **Lieutenant Colonel Charles Boote** (II.B.12), a pre-war territorial and manager of a pottery in Staffordshire, who had been in command of 1/6 North Staffordshires for less than a month, lies along with forty-eight identified men of his regiment who were killed with him on 1 July 1916. Many

Gommecourt Wood New Cemetery.

more must lie amongst the unidentified. **Private Charles Sergeant** (I.G.24) was only 18 when he enlisted in Grimsby in 1915. He took part in the 46th Division attack on the Hohenzollern Redoubt in September 1915 where he was wounded serving with 1/5 Lincolnshires. He was killed at about midnight on 1 July when his company was ordered to make contact with the already dead or captured Sherwood Foresters.

Lieutenant Colonel Charles Boote.

Also buried here is **Private Edward Whitlock** (IV.B.4) of 1/4 Ox and Bucks Light Infantry who was the first man to be killed after British troops took over the sector in 1915. Whitlock, who enlisted in Oxford, was killed by a shell on 22 July 1915 near Hébuterne. A memorial on the cemetery wall near the entrance commemorates the actions of the 46th Division on 1 July 1916. Before you leave pause for a moment at the headstone of 22-year-old **Sergeant Sydney Hibbert** (Sp Mem 5) who was killed fighting with 1/5 South Staffordshires on 1 July 1916. Born in Walsall, he attended Queen Mary's Grammar School where he served in the OTC and was later apprenticed to the Old Park Works in Wednesbury. Leave the cemetery and turn right to return to your vehicle.

Foncquevillers Military Cemetery

The cemetery contains 648 Commonwealth casualties, of which 53 are unidentified, and special memorials to 2 casualties known to be buried amongst them are located to the left of the entrance. The five aircrew of Halifax LW135 are also buried here along with four Germans. Started by the French, the first British burial was 30-year-old **Private William Bradley** (II.D.2) who was killed serving with 10/Royal Fusiliers on

To reach **Foncquevillers Military Cemetery**, take the D6 past Gommecourt Wood New British Cemetery to arrive at the crossroads with the D3 in the centre of Foncquevillers. Cross straight over into the Rue Bacon following the CWGC signposts. The cemetery is at the far end of the road. The village also has a cafe/restaurant near the *Mairie* and two plaques commemorating the North Staffordshires at the base of the war memorial. Next to the church is a more recent memorial to the crew of Halifax LW135 of 427 Squadron which crashed during the night of 13 June 1944, the remains of one engine being displayed nearby.

Two plaques commemorating the North Staffordshires stand at the base of the Foncquevillers village war memorial.

The memorial to the crew of Halifax LW135 that stands outside the church at Foncquevillers.

6 September 1915. Another pre-1 July 1916 casualty buried here is **Private Arthur Lomas** (1.G.16), a great friend of Thomas Higgins and killed on the night of 23/24 June 1916 whilst in the covering party for those digging the advanced trench in no-man's-land. Casualties of 1 July are buried in a mass grave at the rear of the cemetery where there are as many as three names on a single headstone.

Buried close by is **Captain John Green** (III.D.15), the RAMC officer who was killed on 1 July 1916. He was the only man of the 46th Division to be awarded the **Victoria Cross** on that day, although his body was not recovered until the spring of 1917. His widow received his cross from King George V in October 1916. Green's younger brother, **Second Lieutenant Edward Green**, had been killed at Loos in 1915. Several other 1/7 Sherwood Forester casualties of 1 July were brought in during March 1917; 23-year-old **Captain William Walker** (III.E.6) and 18-year-old **Second Lieutenants Wilfred Flint** (III.E.5) and Leicester-born **Frank Gamble** (III.E.4) lie side by side, whilst 23-year-old **Captain Thomas Leman** (III.D.10) – who, shot in the arm and jaw and dying between the first and second German lines, ordered the men with him to try to escape – may well have been recovered at a later date.

Before you leave visit the graves of two young men – both killed on 1 July 1916 – from different backgrounds who lie close together. 19-year-old **Second Lieutenant William Callard** (I.L.15) of the 1/5 Leicesters taught in the Bishop Street Methodist Sunday School and had just won a scholarship to Oxford University when he joined up. He was killed by a shell whilst waiting to counter-attack and is one of twenty-three members of the congregation whose names are inscribed on the church memorial. 19-year-old Derby-born **Private Bertram 'Bertie' Cheadle** (I.L.17) of the 1/5 Sherwood Foresters left school at 14 to work in the motor industry and enlisted in March 1915. Amongst the personal effects that were returned to George and Sarah Cheadle after his death were a wallet, letters, photos, a fountain pen and a figure of Christ.

Captain John Leslie Green was the only recipient of the Victoria Cross at Gommecourt.

Route 2

Gommecourt South

A circular tour beginning at: the *Mairie*
Coordinates: 50°08′21.35″ N – 2°38′43.11″ E
Distance: 5.8km/3.6 miles
Suitable for: 🚶 🚵
Grade: Easy (total ascent 44m)
Maps: IGN Série Bleue 2407O — Acheux-en-Amiénois

General description and context: This route has been designed in conjunction with **Route 1** and looks at the 56th Division attack of 1 July 1916, visiting five CWGC cemeteries en route. The 900m-long front of the 56th Division followed a line from the southern edge of Gommecourt Park to a point called '16 Poplars' on the D27 Hébuterne–Puisieux road. Faced with a no-man's-land some 750m wide in certain places, **Major General Charles Hull**, commanding the division, ordered a new jumping-off trench to be dug to reduce the distance to the German line. It was a Herculean effort and the trench was dug but attempts to push it

Major General Charles Hull.

forward still further were abandoned because of poor weather. The two assaulting brigades – **169 Brigade** on the left flank just south of the Chemin de Gommecourt and **168 Brigade** to its right, astride the Rue de Bucquoy – were supported by **167 Brigade** which was held in reserve around Hébuterne. The German defences opposite the 56th Division were garrisoned by IR 170 with four companies from RIR 55. The **Kern Redoubt** garrison was largely made up of RIR 55, IR 170 and IR 15.

At 7.20am on 1 July smoke was discharged from the left of the British front line which quickly enveloped the whole position allowing the assault to proceed as planned 10 minutes later. The enemy wire had largely been cut by the preliminary bombardment and the advance waves of Londoners soon overpowered the men in the German first-line trenches and moved forward into the third line. Small groups of 16/Queen's Westminster Rifles (QWR) reached **The Quadrilateral** by bombing their way along **Ems Trench** where they were due to meet up with units from the 46th Division.

This initial success could not be maintained. There is no doubt that the crushing failure of the 46th Division attack had disastrous consequences for the progress of the 56th Division battalions, which found themselves repeatedly fending off counter-attacks from troops who had been diverted from their defences north and east of Gommecourt in order to bolster the defence. The situation was compounded by German machine-gun and artillery fire which severely reduced the reinforcement of men and ammunition across no-man's-land. Cut off and with dwindling stocks of ammunition, the British lodgement in the German line came under increasing pressure. By 4.00pm the Germans had retaken their second-line trenches and had regained a footing in their own front line and inexorably snuffed out the Londoners' resistance, many being either killed or captured. By 10.00pm that evening the German lines were once more clear of British troops, leaving those still alive in no-man's-land to run a gauntlet of fire back to their own lines. The cost of the 56th Division's assault in casualties was 3,263 officers and men killed, wounded and missing.

Directions to start: Gommecourt is situated on the D6 between Foncquevillers and Puisieux. Park outside the *Mairie*.

Route description: With the *Mairie* on your right continue through the village bearing right at the fork – signposted 'D6 Puisieux and Miraumont' – to take the first turning on the right. This is the Rue d'Hébuterne **Ⓐ** which runs down the eastern edge of Gommecourt Park and cuts through the former site of the **Kern Redoubt**. In 1916 the park was more of an ornamental addition to Gommecourt Chateau, today it is a wood which unfortunately is private property but still contains the remnants of the old German trench systems, some of which you may be able to see through the foliage.

The road hugs the bulk of Gommecourt Park but some 200m after passing a large farm complex on the left and rounding a bend, the tree line veers off to the right and the view opens up to your left to reveal the ground over which 169 Brigade attacked. The German front line skirted the edge of Gommecourt Park – to your right – then switched 90 degrees to cross the road from right to left here and ran out across the fields to your left – the first three sections of trenches named **Fen**, **Ferret** and **Fern** respectively by the British – before heading south

Looking north along the Rue d'Hébuterne towards Gommecourt with Gommecourt Park Wood on the left.

towards Serre. Also to your left and across the field you should be able to see **Gommecourt Communal Cemetery** ❸ on the Rue St-Martin which was situated between the second and third German lines. Later during the morning of 1 July, after the German counter-attacks, this ground, pitted with shell holes, would have been a scene of carnage as groups of wounded men attempted to find their way back to British lines through a hail of German machine-gun and artillery fire. As the Rue d'Hébuterne bends round to the right the spire of Hébuterne church soon comes into view and on your far left, marked by the clump of trees, **Gommecourt British Cemetery No. 2** should be visible. Look up the slope to your right. As you get level with, then pass the tip of, Gommecourt Park pick out the electricity pylon on the skyline marking the approximate position of the British front line which ran across the fields here and across the road in front of you. ❻ Stop here.

The road you are on approximates the extreme left flank of the 56th Division's attack and if you now turn around and face Gommecourt you will have the same view that the 5/London Regiment (London Rifle Brigade, LRB) had as they attacked in six waves astride the road towards the point you have just passed, where the trees of the Park left the road. Commanded by **Lieutenant Colonel Arthur Bates** and plagued by machine-gun fire from the Park, they initially overcame the German front-line defences before being forced back to their own lines. It was from **Eck Trench**, just behind the German second line, that **Second**

Lieutenant Robert Petley of D Company, LRB, sent a runner back to British lines late in the afternoon with a request for more bombs. This group whom he describes as 'several officers and about 60 or 70 men' may well have been the last British troops still in German lines. At 9.45pm, seizing their chance to get across no-man's-land under the cover of the gathering dusk, the group left **Ferret Trench** and started out on the hazardous journey back to British lines. 'Most of the party, I am afraid, were hit in no man's land' wrote Petley, who survived the encounter with a small wound to the knee and the award of the Military Cross.

    Sergeant Harold Bisgood of 2/London Regiment (Royal Fusiliers) crossed this same ground to your right later on during the afternoon of 1 July as part of his battalion followed up the initial attack of the LRB and 9/London Regiment (Queen Victoria's Rifles, QVR). The previous day he had noted in his diary that he expected it to be a 'walk-over as our guns have not been replied to and barely a German has been seen'. He later recorded the opening of the attack:

> At last the long looked for day and hour has arrived; broad daylight, the rain has ceased and the day is quite bright. The din now is beyond all imagination, every gun in France seems to be turned on the Hun on our front: surely none can live in this hail of shells. Meanwhile all our front line men had been engaged in lighting smoke candles and firing huge smoke bombs. Now arises a dense cloud of smoke all along our line and the time has arrived when we must show our hands and advance. The Germans as soon as they saw the smoke knew what was to follow and rapid fire was opened at once. Nothing daunted, the London boys climbed up the parapet ready for the fray; they advanced in the face of terrible fire … Men fell by the dozen, yet … the remainder pushed on. Only a small percentage of each regiment ever got into the German trenches [and] these few gallantly hacked their way right into the 3rd line from where they sent us the SOS signal.

At 1.45pm Bisgood's 'walk' began.

    Picture yourself for a moment standing beside Sergeant Bisgood as he went over the top. His description of the advance of A and C companies across no-man's-land in support of the LRB and QVR leaves little to the imagination:

> We, the 2nd London were the reserve … and as soon as the battalions in front sent the signal two companies were up and over

despite the fact that all fire was now concentrated on our particular sectors. The sight of our boys advancing in the face of this terrible fire was wonderful though terrible; losses in our two companies alone numbered 250. Our trenches were now blocked with dead and dying, only a dozen or so of our lads ever reached Fritz's trenches at all, hundreds were lying in no man's land mostly dead, some however alive though badly wounded managed to crawl into shell holes of which there were thousands.

Imagine now the noise of battle coming from the German lines as Sergeant Bisgood and his men fought to hold on in the German lines until about 7.00pm when all their ammunition ran out. Imagine German shells exploding all around you here, making it impossible to cross no-man's-land and re-supply the embattled Londoners. Under ferocious counter attack, Bisgood and his dwindling band were compelled to fall back:

first from the 3rd German line, then from the 2nd into the 1st and finally the 100 or so that were left had to retire over the top towards our own lines. What a horrible journey midst a hail of bullets, past heaps of dead and dying eventually (with only twenty-seven instead of the 100 odd that started) covered in mud and blood. Twenty-three of the twenty-seven badly wounded.

He then witnessed an amazing sight near this spot:

Suddenly at about 7.30 pm the firing died down … and looking out I noticed a man had boldly climbed out of the German trench and was holding up a large white board with a brilliant red cross painted on it. This man advanced well into the centre of no man's land and beckoned to us, whereupon one of our stretcher bearers jumped over the parapet and went to meet him. The man with the board was a German doctor who spoke quite good English; he offered an Armistice of one hour and this after much ado was accepted by our people. The Hun doctor then signalled with his hand and immediately a party of about fifty German stretcher bearers doubled out and started attending to the wounded. This was good enough for us and over we went again … The Germans were real bricks and kept their word to the letter, extending the armistice ten minutes to allow us time to get into our trenches again. Our people however did not play the game as after we had been out about half an hour they put some shells right into the

German lines. We thought our time had come and said goodbye to each other, but still the Hun kept his promise and not a shot was fired, this little episode made us feel awful cads.

By now many walking wounded were trooping out of the British communication trenches like the crowd from a football match. Already choked with the dead and dying these trenches – in 'Y sector' so with names beginning with 'Y' – ran parallel to the road here in the fields to either side. Young Street was 250m away as you look towards Gommecourt Park whilst Yiddish and Yellow Streets were to the south some 120m and 220m away respectively. Sergeant Bisgood was with the Londons' recovery party:

> Most of the wounded we found in shell holes, I found three chums in a hole all unable to move but cuddled together ... The look of amazement and relief on the poor devils faces when they saw us peering over the shell hole was good to see. One boy could not believe it and asked me amid sobs if he was dreaming. I am glad to be able to write and say that we got all our wounded in. The dead we could do nothing for, as time would not permit. I covered over a few of the most hideous cases and returned to the line sick, sad and very fatigued.

He then came across more gruesome scenes:

> a tableau of three of my chums [in Young Street] one standing, one sitting (headless) and the other lying, all three had been hit by the same shell. In the dusk in Yiddish Street I stumbled over something and bending down to my horror found it was a man's head ... In Yellow Street I was clutched at and caught by a hand protruding from the side of the trench, all that was visible was a hand and arm, the sleeve showed it to be an officer of the LRBs.

2/Londons were finally relieved next day and straggled in 'penny numbers' to Sailly-au-Bois where they were shelled heavily and Bisgood recalled that 'every moment, I expected one to drop through my house (a tin-roofed hut). I shall always remember this night, I completely broke down.'

Before continuing look into the field to the south. Many of the London Division dead of 1 July 1916 were buried in or just behind the British front line in this vicinity and according to CWGC records the body of an unknown second lieutenant of 1/5 Cheshires, the Pioneer battalion of the 56th Division, was found buried under a cross 50m into the field here along with the bodies of Privates William Poole (also 5/Cheshires), Leonard Collis (QVR) and another unidentified QVR. We shall return to the story of the 'unknown' Cheshires officer later.

Our route now climbs gently into the village of Hébuterne – Bisgood's battalion advanced from a position near the trees on the outskirts of the village and down the slope to your left – and the T-junction with the D28. At the T-junction you can either turn left through the village to continue the route or take the opportunity to visit the British observation post which you will find some 440m along the D6 to the right **❶**. The concrete structure can be found near a calvary on the right-hand side of the road, set back some 60m in the corner of a small field. It was constructed in 1918 by the 42nd Divisional Engineers.

Retrace your steps past the T-junction to the first of the two village greens and stop. In 1916 the smaller of the two greens boasted a pond which was filled in after the war when Hébuterne was adopted by Evesham – the 48th (South Midland) Division was here during 1915. The village gave its name to an action fought by the French in June 1915 during the Second Battle of Artois before it was taken over by British troops. Given its proximity to the German lines, the village was continually harassed by German shell fire which accounts for the village green being known as **Shell Green** by the troops.

The British observation post on the D28 north of Hébuterne.

Hébuterne Military Cemetery ❺ is best approached from the village green by following the CWGC signposts along the D27 Rue de Sailly for 300m where a right turn up a metalled track will take you to the entrance. Here you will find sixty-one casualties from 1 July 1916. Begun in an orchard by ambulance units of the 48th Division in 1915, it was used by the 56th Division until the spring of 1917. There are now over 750 casualties buried here and of these nearly 50 are unidentified. Special memorials are erected to seventeen soldiers known or believed to be buried amongst them. You will also find three German graves at the rear of the cemetery. In Plot 4, Row M, next to the Stone of Remembrance, are sixty-one casualties killed on 1 July whose names have been shared amongst twenty-one headstones. There are a number of 17-year-olds buried here but the only one killed on 1 July was **Private Frank Corbell** (II.Q.9) from Walthamstow who was serving with 3/London Regiment. Probably the most well-known individual buried here is 37-year-old **Captain Richard Seddon** (I.F.1) who is amongst the fifty-three New Zealand casualties from 1918 scattered around the cemetery. Seddon was killed on 21 August 1918 serving with the New Zealand Rifle Brigade and was the son of the Right Hon. Richard 'King Dick' Seddon who was the longest serving Prime Minister of New Zealand (1893–1906). Buried next to each other are **Lieutenant Edward Carre** (I.H.6) and **Sergeant Fred Barton** (I.H.5) who were shot down by German ace Oswald Boelcke on 16 October flying a BE2d from 15 Squadron which was operating in support of IV Corps from the airfield at Marieux. Before you leave spare a moment for **Private Milson Parr** (I.V.9) who died on 12 October 1916 serving with 51/Battalion, Machine Gun Corps. He was one of three brothers who were killed during the war; 18-year-old Sapper Stanley Parr served in the Royal Engineers and died of pneumonia at home on 26 February 1915 and 30-year-old Lance Corporal George Parr was killed fighting with 8/KRRC on 16 September 1916. You will find George's name on the Thiepval Memorial. A fourth brother, Corporal Joseph Parr, serving with the Lancashire Hussars, survived the war.

Retrace your route to the village green and follow the CWGC signpost directing you along the Rue de Bucquoy to Gommecourt British Cemetery No. 2. This leads you out of the village along a narrow minor road parallel to the line of **Wurzel Street**, a long communication trench that ran to the left of the road and hosted an

Captain Richard Seddon.

advanced dressing station during the 1 July attack. After some 500m you should be able to get a clear view across to Gommecourt Park and the open ground over which 169 Brigade attacked.

Ahead of you – in no-man's-land – is the Cross of Sacrifice of Gommecourt British Cemetery No. 2. You should also be able to see Gommecourt Communal Cemetery ❸ across to the left which was behind the German second line as it ran from your right across to Gommecourt Park. As the road descends along the original 1916 route you will cross the British front line about 100m before reaching the path ❶ leading to the cemetery on the left, but before you enter imagine a track forking off into the fields to your right with a single 'Lone Tree' standing at the junction. It was from this point that 12/London Regiment (The Rangers) – the left assault battalion of 168 Brigade – attacked astride the road ahead towards the German lines.

Gommecourt British Cemetery No. 2 sits between the two opposing front lines and from the rear wall you can look out over the fields across which the left flank companies of The Rangers attacked. Gommecourt British Cemeteries No. 1, No. 2, No. 3 and No. 4 were begun in 1917 when the battlefields were cleared. No. 2 originally contained 101 graves of 1 July 1916, almost all from the 56th Division, these casualties form Plot I of the cemetery as it is today. Plot 4, Row M contains graves from 1 July 1916, each headstone having several names inscribed on it. Typical of these is 18-year-old **Rifleman Oscar Howard** (I.A.5) who shares a headstone with 19-year-old **Rifleman Sidney Smith**. Both boys were serving with 12/Londons – The Rangers. Along the right-hand wall are twenty-seven headstones of men believed to be buried in the cemetery including 26-year-old **Lieutenant John Brown-Constable** (II.G.26), who was born in India and worked in Pretoria prior to the outbreak of war in 1914. Commanding D Company, London Scottish, he was killed on 1 July in the vicinity of **Farmyard Trench** some 600m away to the southeast. Spare a moment for 21-year-old **Private Edwin Carlton** (II.D.26) who was killed in the same attack and joined the Leeds University Officer Training Corps prior to enlisting in the London Scottish in December 1915. He had only been in France for a month. Brothers 20-year-old **Rifleman Phillip Bassett** (III.B.12) and 25-year-old **Rifleman Henry Bassett** (III.B.13) are buried next to each other. Both boys were killed on 1 July serving with QVR. Two company commanders from Sergeant Harold Bisgood's 2/London Regiment – 23-year-old **Captain James Garland** (III.H.1) of A Company and 37-year-old **Captain Percy Handyside** (II.L.11) of C Company – were both killed within half an hour of each other whilst attempting to cross no-man's-land on the afternoon of 1 July. Before leaving find

Gommecourt British Cemetery No. 2 looking over the ground across which 169 Brigade attacked on 1 July.

and note Special Memorial D (III.C.15) to **Second Lieutenant George Stuart Arthur** of 1/5 Cheshire Regiment. The memorial is linked to the discovery of the body of the unidentified second lieutenant of the Cheshires south of the Gommecourt–Hébuterne road, almost at the point **●** where you stopped earlier. We shall return to Arthur's story later.

Before you leave the cemetery slowly scan the fields all around it. When the Germans pulled back to the Hindenburg Line in February 1917 and the British followed them up, they came across the remains of many who had been cut down in no-man's-land near here almost eight months earlier and had never been recovered. One of the soldiers serving on this sector at the time was **Richard Sparling,** a sports journalist who had enlisted in the Sheffield City Battalion (12/York and Lancaster Regiment) in 1914. Sparling had fought at Serre and had survived the destruction of his beloved City Battalion on 1 July 1916 (see **Route 3**) and in 1920 wrote its official history. Now imagine the scene as you read Sparling's description of the gruesome tableaux that greeted the British troops crossing the old no-man's-land to north and south of this very spot in early 1917:

What a 'Promised Land' they found as they followed the enemy up! ... Numerous skeletons lay there in long rows, with their equipment on just as they had fallen in the fights of July 1st ... The gaunt, spiritless trees of Gommecourt [Park] ... had been silent witnesses of slaughter. The bodies lay in all kinds of positions – some very straight, some doubled up, some with arms folded, some with legs doubled under them, some with legs crossed. Heads were loose, and some had rolled from their trunks.

Another man wrote of being alarmed at his callousness on finding that he had noted 'the fact of rats having fed on the bodies without the slightest feeling of sentiment'. He went on to record how 'the teeth in the skulls gleamed in the sunshine' and that 'some of the skulls still had patches of hair, red hair and black hair, adhering to them'. He remarked how the men's trousers and boots 'looked as if packed with sawdust, and how one man's crumbling thigh-bone resembled the brown musty edges of a century-old volume'.

Another City Battalion survivor of 1 July was **Lance Corporal Reg Glenn**. He, the padre Frank Ford – a family friend – and an officer went out to the German wire near here in March 1917 and turned to look back at the British line. 'Then the padre said a prayer for the dead and we sang "For All the Saints". Next morning the dead were buried by an overnight fall of snow.' The anonymous officer later wrote a poem – 'The Heroes of ... Tree' – which Frank Ford sent to Reg Glenn's parents in a letter. Given that Glenn's group were on this very sector at the time the missing word is almost certainly 'Lone' and so that poignant vignette was played out here.

> There they lay, as for months they had lain,
> In 'No man's land' of the Picardy Plain
> In two long waves by the German wire
> Advancing, caught by machine gun fire.
> With bowed head and lips closed tight
> We passed, deep moved by the tragic sight,
> Then, voicing the wish of the rest, one said
> 'Oh, Padre, pray for these heroes dead'.
> At break of dawn, to our surprise
> The world was white before our eyes;
> A mighty hand in answer spread
> a pure white mantle o'er the dead.

After 250m you will cross the German front line – known as **Fate Trench** by the British – which ran left to right across the road in front of you. Between this point and the crossroads up ahead were three distinct lines of German trenches complete with two belts of barbed wire. On your right is the ground over which 168 Brigade attacked, whilst 12/London Regiment (The Rangers) attacked along the line of the road you are now on with the 14/London Regiment (The London Scottish), commanded by **Lieutenant Colonel Bernard Green**, to their right with its A Company practically on the D27 Hébuterne–Puisieux road close to a clump of trees known as **16 Poplars**. **Private Henry Smith** was with 8 Platoon, B Company of the London Scottish and was one of the few in his platoon to survive the encounter:

> 8 Platoon leading the company reached the German front line to find our bombardment had driven them back to their second line. Went on to their second line. Tremendous hand-to-hand fighting and here I killed my first German – shot him clean through the forehead and sent his hat spinning in the air. Just afterwards I killed two more. Bombs and bullets by the thousand and the ground blowing up under our feet. Awful sights and fearful casualties.

Of the 856 officers and men of the London Scottish who had gone in to action only 9 officers and 257 other ranks survived.

At the crossroads **G** stop. Ahead of you is **Rossignol Wood** from which German machine guns poured a torrent of fire into the advancing Rangers on 1 July and where the 1/5 and 1/6 North Staffordshires from the 46th Division attacked on 14 March 1917. **Tommy Higgins** – by now a lance corporal – remembered the disastrous assault during which 133 men – including Tommy's mate Lance Corporal Frank Harrison – were killed or missing. Harrison is buried at Shrine Cemetery, Bucquoy. Should you wish to visit **Rossignol Wood Cemetery** a short 200m detour to the right along the D6 will be necessary where you will find thirty-four men from the North Staffordshires' attack buried in the first two rows of graves. The cemetery was begun in March 1917 and the German plot was added after the Armistice when graves were brought in from the battlefields immediately to the south and southwest. The cemetery now contains seventy German war graves – forty-two of them being unidentified – mainly from the 1918 fighting, although those who fought with II/IR 170 were victims of the 1916 fighting.

Further along the road is the tiny **Owl Trench Cemetery** which contains fifty-three burials all of whom, with the exception of **Private Leonard Hainsworth**, were killed on 27 February 1917 during another abortive raid on Rossignol Wood by 16/West Yorks (1st Bradford Pals). Ten of the burials in the cemetery are unidentified.

Leave the cemetery and retrace your steps to the crossroads and continue along the D6 towards Gommecourt for approximately 500m. On the left of the road here were the ruins of **Nameless Farm**, a German stronghold which has long since ceased to exist but was positioned facing the wall of Gommecourt Cemetery No. 2. Known by the Germans as **Bock Farm,** it was one of the objectives of The Rangers and from its ruins a deadly machine-gun fire was brought to bear on them. Heavily defended, it resisted all attempts by the Londoners to capture the position. Even before the men of C Company crossed the German second line they were under heavy fire from both the farm and Rossignol Wood and handicapped by the uncut wire which remained a serious obstacle. Eventually managing to break through the uncut wire into the German second line, C Company, despite reinforcements from 4/London Regiment (Royal Fusiliers), found their progress effectively halted.

Continue along the road to the communal cemetery and stop. Eck communication trench, which skirted the southern perimeter of the cemetery before running across the road and into the fields to the northwest, linked the second German line with their third. Turn and look into the fields opposite the cemetery gates. Eck Trench merged with Ems Trench after about 100m and the latter culminated in The Quadrilateral position, which was 400m beyond. Imagine the bombers of the QWR out in the fields as they fought their way past the cemetery at about 8.30am and along Ems Trench accompanied by men of A Company of the 5th (Earl of Chester's) Battalion The

The tiny Owl Trench Cemetery which contains fifty-three burials.

Cheshire Regiment (1/5 Cheshires), the divisional pioneers, who were to construct a strongpoint running through Ems Trench to the cemetery and consolidate The Quadrilateral. With all their own officers out of action the QWR bombers were in fact led by a 32-year-old Cheshires officer whose name is not noted in the QWR war diary but who Martin Middlebrook identified as Bristol-born Second Lieutenant George Stuart Arthur in his *First Day on the Somme*. Arthur, a draper working for his father in Halifax, West Yorkshire before the war, was commissioned from the ranks on 6 March 1915. He was last seen leading the attack as his party bombed its way 400m down the German trench across the field in front of you almost to the point where they should have linked up with the leading men of the northern pincer of the 46th Division. Instead, they found only Germans. In the fierce bombing duel which ensued, the Londoners ran out of bombs and after half an hour Arthur ordered his men back and stayed to cover their retirement, facing the Germans alone with his revolver. Some sources record that Arthur was never seen again but a sergeant of 1/5 Cheshires stated that he saw Arthur in the German front line just before they made a dash for it, which might explain the location of the grave near the spot, south of the Gommecourt–Hébuterne road – which you visited earlier – where the body of a second lieutenant of the Cheshires was buried. When the bodies were exhumed to be concentrated in larger cemeteries in the early 1920s, the unknown Cheshires officer was moved to Gommecourt British Cemetery No. 2, also visited earlier. As Arthur was the only 5/Cheshires second lieutenant to go missing on 1 July 1916 the grave marker was changed in 1996 from that of an unknown officer of the Cheshire Regiment to a special memorial bearing his name.

It was somewhere here in Gommecourt Communal Cemetery that Private Lancashire, also of 5/Cheshires, saw his platoon commander, 21-year-old Jersey-born Philip Burnet Bass, badly wounded in a 'friendly fire' incident:

> My platoon under Lieutenant Bass was ordered to consolidate the cemetery … We got the order to advance and got bombed … so we got down and opened fire near the German front line trench. I looked to my right and saw Lieutenant Bass with Private [John Emmanuel] Clifford going over some high ground near the German second line … I made my way to him [and he] gave orders to three of us … to make a fire step in a trench running through the cemetery. As we were digging, some bombers passed along and one accidentally dropped a bomb which exploded. Lieutenant Bass was hit in the eye and Clifford was wounded. We bandaged

them up but could not stop Lieutenant Bass bleeding and I went to find someone to report to.

It is said that Private Clifford volunteered and set out to carry Bass back to the British lines but that was the last anyone saw of them. Both men are remembered on the Thiepval Memorial. The remaining parties of 169 Brigade's mixed lodgement of QWR and QVR in this vicinity were finally driven out of the German lines by 8.30pm. Leave the cemetery and turn left towards Gommecourt and as you do so you will traverse the inner fortifications of the Kern Redoubt from south to north as you reach the *Mairie* to return to your vehicle.

Front Line Spine Route
Gommecourt to Serre

Distance: 8.6km/5.3 miles
Suitable for: 🚗 🚲

From Gommecourt follow the D6 towards Puisieux passing the communal cemetery on the right. You are now following the line of the third German line for a short stretch here, passing the site of Nameless Farm after 550m and taking the next right – Rue de Bucqoy – at the green CWGC sign. This road passes **Gommecourt British Cemetery No. 2**, which was visited in **Route 2**.

Continue on this road to the T-junction approximately 1km ahead where you will see the village green and a familiar CWGC signpost which directs you to **Hébuterne Communal Cemetery**. The cemetery is at the southern extremity of Hébuterne and can be found by turning left, continuing past the village green and taking the first road on the right after the church – Rue de l'Eglise. Follow the road round for 500m and the communal cemetery is on your left. The cemetery register is lodged at the *Mairie*. The cemetery was taken over by the British from the French in 1915. It was again the scene of fighting in March 1918 when the New Zealand Division held up the German advance. Today the cemetery contains two plots of graves containing fifty-six British and fifty-four French casualties, none of which are casualties of 1 July 1916. One of two brothers, **Second Lieutenant Percy Fisher** DCM (I.A.8) was 34 years old when he was killed on 12 September 1916 serving with the 22/Royal Fusiliers. His younger brother, 33-year-old Captain Raymond Fisher, was killed 24 hours later on 13 September 1916 in Salonika whilst attached to Army Headquarters. Before you leave pause for a moment by the grave of Surrey-born 18-year-old **Sergeant Leonard Tamplin** (I.B.14) who was killed serving in D Company, 17/Royal Fusiliers, on 28 September 1916. Both battalions of Fusiliers fought at **Delville Wood** in July 1916.

After visiting the cemetery, retrace your route back to the church and turn right at the T-junction onto the D27 signed Pusieux, then bear right at the triangular green to take the single-track road – Rue de Serre. You are about to pass from the southern flank of Lieutenant General Edmund

Allenby's Third Army sector into the most northerly sector of Rawlinson's Fourth Army; essentially a 'gap' of one mile. Here there would be no attack on 1 July 1916, the gap being filled by two line-holding battalions of 143 Brigade of the 48th Division. It was a gap that understandably preyed on the mind of the Third Army commander.

Continue and bear left at the fork ahead to pass a large farm complex on the left – **New Touvent Farm**. Slow down here as a glance across to the right will reveal the clump of trees marking the site of the copses that took the name of the four Evangelists, Matthew, Mark, Luke and John (John being nearest the road), which we will visit in **Route 3**. Some 700m before the road enters the village of Serre – which was adopted by the City of Sheffield after the war – you pass **Pierrard Farm** on the right. Continue to the T-junction and turn right onto the D919, as you leave the village slow down to find the **Memorial to the Sheffield City Battalion** (12/York and Lancaster Regiment) on the right where you will find parking. The memorial was designed by Augustin Rey and unveiled on 21 May 1923 in the presence of veterans who had fought at Serre in 1916. Several prominent individuals from Sheffield were present at the ceremony, including **Herbert Jones,** who had been Archdeacon of Sheffield during the war and who dedicated the memorial. At the time this memorial had the distinction of being the only battalion memorial on the Western Front. Several books written since the 1970s repeat the British Official History's assertion that a few men from 12/York and Lancaster Regiment reached the northwest corner of Serre on 1 July 1916 as their bodies were found during the unsuccessful attack of 13 November 1916 when the 3rd Division briefly entered the village, but contemporary German sources do not support this theory. They could just as well have been found dead in the German first line – or wounded and taken prisoner, only to die shortly afterwards – and then have been buried in Serre.

The village resisted all attempts at capture until 24 February 1917 when the Germans retired to the **Hindenburg Line** and 21/Manchesters moved up and occupied it by 10.10am the following day

The Sheffield City Battalion (12/York and Lancaster Regiment) Memorial in Serre.

losing only 1 man killed and 5 wounded; exactly 3,594 fewer casualties than the attempt on 1 July 1916 had incurred!

In a little over 1km you will see **Serre Road Cemetery No. 1** on your right and **Serre Road Cemetery No. 2** another 500m further along the road on the left. Park here. We suggest you visit Serre Road Cemetery No. 2 after completing the route.

Route 3

Serre

A circular tour beginning at: **Serre Road Cemetery No. 2**
Coordinates: 50°05′48.06″ N – 2°39′04.73″ E
Distance: 5.2km/3.2 miles
Suitable for: ⸙
Grade: Moderate (total ascent 44m)
Maps: IGN Série Bleue 2407O – Acheux-en-Amiénois

General description and context: This route is probably best completed on foot. Initially the route crosses the left flank of the 4th Division's (**Major General Sir William Lambton**) attack north of the Serre–Mailly-Maillet road (D919). This focused on the *Heidenkopf* – an angular system of trenches dug by Bavarian reinforcements following the bloody Battle of Serre – fought against the French in June 1915.

The 1/8 Royal Warwicks (48th Division loaned to 4th Division) entered the *Heidenkopf* with little opposition on the extreme left, despite the detonation of four mines the Germans had prepared for such an eventuality. The 1/8 Warwicks advanced into the neighbouring support trenches under heavy fire from the northeast and gained a feeble hold on the fourth German line before being driven back to the third. Supporting battalions were ordered up at 7.40am including 1/6 Royal Warwicks (also 48th Division), which, despite having eighty casualties before it had cleared its own lines, must have suffered more casualties from the German mines, which, according to Jack Sheldon's research into German official sources, were blown at roughly the same time. The survivors pressed on and joined men of their sister battalion in consolidating the latter's gains before pushing on to reach what eventually seemed like, to **Second Lieutenant George Wright Glover** of the Rifle Brigade at least, 'a most awful jumble … of every regiment in the division' fighting hard in the fourth line.

But with both the attacks on Serre and the Redan Ridge to north and south stalling in the face of stiff opposition, the Warwicks in and around the *Heidenkopf* were gradually forced to give ground until around 7.30pm – some 12 hours after the attack had begun – the surviving troops were forced to withdraw to the British lines. Others retired after dark and a

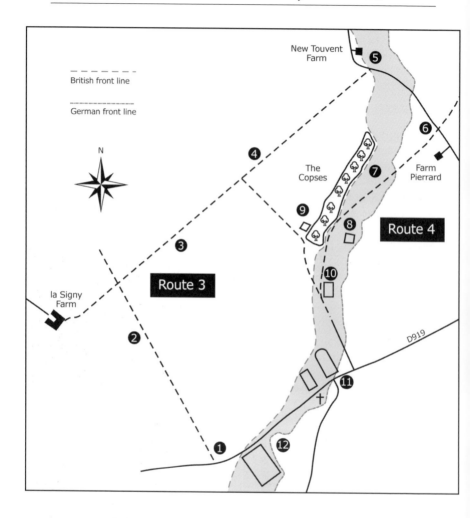

company of 1/Royal Irish Fusiliers even held on until around 11.30am next morning before coming back.

We then move on to look at the 31st Division's (Major General Robert Wanless-O'Gowan) attack on Serre where the front line ran along the front of four small copses with **John Copse** situated on the extreme left of the divisional – and thus the entire Fourth Army – attack. At 7.30am the assaulting battalions of 93 and 94 Brigades, made up almost entirely of unseasoned Kitchener Pals battalions from the towns and cities of the industrial heartland of Yorkshire and Lancashire, began their advance across no-man's-land to be met by a murderous hail of machine-gun and artillery fire which cut swathes of them down before they had advanced more than a few metres. The assault was an unmitigated disaster and the division suffered 1,349 killed and 2,169 wounded. Many English towns and cities in northern counties were left mourning in the aftermath, the memory of which is partly responsible for the many permanent memorials that still exist today in Sheffield Memorial Park.

Directions to start: Park outside Serre Road Cemetery No. 2, which you can approach along the D919 running between Mailly-Maillet and Puisieux.

Route description: After parking your vehicle outside Serre Road Cemetery No. 2 walk back along the road towards Serre Road Cemetery No. 1, which you can see ahead of you on the left. After some 50m you will find the memorial cross to 20-year-old **Lieutenant Valentine Ashworth Braithwaite** MC situated near the northern corner of the cemetery. Commemorated on the Thiepval Memorial, this young Winchester School educated officer joined 1/Somersets on the Aisne in September 1914 and was one of the first recipients of the then newly instituted Military Cross in early 1915 for defending a barricade – a mere cart across the road – during a sustained German attack near St Yves (Yvon), Ploegsteert Wood, on 30 October 1914, laughing openly at the suggestion that he couldn't make ground to the besieged barricade with a 'come on boys' as he led his men forward. He was also Mentioned in Despatches. He was killed during the attack on the *Heidenkopf* ⑫ which was situated in the fields behind and to the left of the memorial. This is the second of two crosses to be erected in his memory on a 1,000m² plot of land purchased by his father, Walter Pipon Braithwaite – ex-Chief of Staff to Sir Ian Hamilton during the Gallipoli campaign and later GOC 62nd (2nd West Riding) Division and XXII and IX Corps commander – in 1921. The original – a wooden grave marker erected by his family in 1918 somewhere further up the slope behind – is in the crypt of Winchester cathedral where his uncle, Philip Richard Pipon Braithwaite, was canon.

The Braithwaite Memorial Cross.

Lieutenant Valentine Braithwaite.

In these same fields, some 20–5m behind the cross, is the probable site of the dugout described by the poet **Lieutenant Wilfred Owen** of 2/Manchesters in a letter to his mother, Susan, in January 1917. It is believed that a close encounter with a German shell, which exploded at the entrance to a dugout in which Owen and his men were sheltering at the time and blew a man down the steps, became the inspiration for one of his most memorable poems, 'The Sentry'.

We'd found an old Boche dug-out, and he knew,
And gave us hell, for shell on frantic shell
Hammered on top, but never quite burst through.
… but one found our door at last.
Buffeting eyes and breath, snuffing the candles.
And thud! flump! thud! down the steep steps came thumping
And splashing in the flood, deluging muck —
The sentry's body; then his rifle, handles
Of old Boche bombs, and mud in ruck on ruck.

You now have the opportunity to visit a memorial – 120m further along the verge on the same side of the road – to three soldiers who were found near here during archaeological work undertaken by the No Man's Land team in 2003 to discover the site of Wilfred Owen's 1917 dugout. Difficult to spot and without the benefit of any parking for vehicles, the plaque commemorates *Vizefeldwebel* **Albert Thielecke** and *Whermann* **Jacob Hönes** – both serving with RIR 121 – who were killed on 11 and 13 June 1915 respectively during the Battle of Toutvent Farm (Serre), together with an unidentified soldier from the King's Own who was probably killed on 1 July 1916. You will find the memorial on the southern verge of the road between the French memorial chapel and Serre Road Cemetery.

Now turn and walk back towards your vehicle and, keeping the cemetery on your left, walk along the main road for 200m until you see a farm track ❶ on your right. Take the track – known as **Sackville Street on** British trench maps – which rises steadily up the spur through the area of the British support lines of the 4th Division. As you breast the rise stop and turn to look right. On a clear day this spot offers a superb panorama of the battlefields of the 4th and 31st divisions. On 1 July the British front line ran – right to left – from the northwest corner of Serre Road Cemetery No. 2 nearest to you, then crossed the road and cut across the northern edge of the French National Cemetery – marked by the fluttering Tricolore – and Serre Road Cemetery No. 1 before swinging north towards the long clump

The Memorial on the D919 to two German soldiers from IR 121 and an unknown British soldier.

of trees on the horizon to the east marking **Sheffield Memorial Park**. Those trees are all that remain of a large tract of woodland – 3.5km long and 1.3km at its widest point – which covered the entire area here and which ran northeast from 700m west of this point almost to Puisieux-au-Mont beyond Serre. Sackville Street was one of the tracks through the woodland.

Scanning the horizon closely between Serre Road Cemetery No. 1 and Sheffield Memorial Park on a clear day you will glimpse the tops of the white Crosses of Sacrifice of Serre Road Cemetery No. 3 and Queens Cemetery, which mark out no-man's-land on the 31st Division's sector. The *Heidenkopf* – named after **Major Heiden** who commanded two battalions of the 1st Bavarian Corps during the 1915 Battle of Serre – squatted in the sloping fields beyond Serre Road No. 2. The 1/6 Royal Warwicks were in their jumping off trenches to the left and right of the track you are standing on with the 1/8 further east; its right flank almost on the road opposite the cemetery gate. Behind the 1/6 were 1/King's Own and 2/Essex. Historian Jack Sheldon is of the opinion that the *Heidenkopf* feature, jutting out towards the British line here, was not a formidable defensive position: it merely occupied 'dead ground' 750m in front of the more important *Feste Soden* position – named after the commander of the German 26th Reserve Division – in the German fourth line and allowed observation towards Serre. The British unimaginatively dubbed it **The Quadrilateral**, as they did many such four-sided 'angular' trench systems on the Western Front!

Regarded as indefensible by the Germans, the four defensive mines – with an average charge of 1,440kg of explosive – were laid beyond the front-line parapet in order to exploit the *Heidenkopf* as a trap. A skeleton garrison included a firing party of engineers who were to blow the mines when the British attacked. Collecting accounts from surviving members of 1/8 Royal Warwicks, **Brigadier General Walter Ludlow**, the chief recruiting officer for Birmingham, described the battalion's advance over no-man's-land towards the *Heidenkopf* here on 1 July, an attack in which his son, 22-year-old **Captain Stratford Ludlow**, was killed fighting with C Company:

> The battalion moved off to the assault at 7.30am on July 1st in eight successive waves of skirmishers at three paces apart, rifles being carried at the port and bayonets fixed. All the officers were in line with the men, and each carried three bombs, as well as 170 rounds of ammunition, entrenching tools, and spade or pick. In addition, between each of the four double companies in the rear were ten men carrying bombs. No other equipment was carried by the men, except a haversack with two days' rations and water bottle.

As the first waves of Warwicks advanced down the slope and crossed the road towards the vicinity of the *Heidenkopf* there seemed little resistance but the German engineers were prepared. Under the command of *Leutnant der Reserve* Eitel, of 4 *Kompanie*, Reserve *Pionier* Battalion 13, the four mines were detonated with great effect some 10 to 15 minutes into the advance creating craters some 10m deep and 25m across and causing casualties amongst the British ranks from debris thrown up by the explosions. Eitel later wrote that the 'casualty-causing effect could be established from the many British dead who were surrounded by falling debris'. The small German garrison holding the *Heidenkopf* also paid the ultimate price for defending their position. The *Heidenkopf* Salient may have fallen but, as **Arthur Cook** of 1/Somersets recalled as he went over in support on the crest of the slope above the cemetery, the Germans still had the advantage:

> The first line had nearly reached the German front line, when all at once machine-guns opened up all along our front with a murderous fire, and we were caught in the open, with no shelter; fire was directed on us from both flanks, men were falling like ninepins, my platoon officer fell, he was wounded and captured.

My platoon sergeant was killed, which left me in charge of the platoon, this within five minutes of our advance.

The machine-gun fire sweeping the ridge forced the Somersets down the slope towards the road beyond the cemetery and they were sucked into the fighting in the *Heidenkopf*. They lost 464 officers and men – including their commanding officer, **Lieutenant Colonel John Audley Thicknesse** – which was fewer than the 472 casualties suffered by 1/6 Royal Warwicks and the 584 men of 1/8 Royal Warwicks – which also lost its commanding officer, **Lieutenant Colonel Edgar Innes**.

Continue along the track, descending into the dip of a shallow valley which runs for 1km off to your right before curving gently left to run behind the rather steep slope upon which stand the trees of Sheffield Memorial Park. In 1916 the valley provided cover for a trench railway which, crossing the track here, connected the support trenches behind Sheffield Memorial Park with supply and ammunition dumps on the way to the village of Colincamps, 3km to the west, and the broad gauge railway network beyond.

Continue. The track ascends again and after 200m or so crosses what was the divisional boundary separating the 4th and 31st divisions on its way to meet a junction of tracks ahead. You have now passed into the sector held by 93 Brigade and five of its assembly trenches for 1 July – Legend, Maitland, Landguard, Dunmow and Bradford – ran away down the slope to your right in a series of almost parallel terraces for some 300m. Here men of 12/King's Own Yorkshire Light Infantry (KOYLI) Pioneers, 18/Durham Light Infantry (Durham Pals), 18/West Yorks (2nd Bradford Pals) and 16/West Yorks (1st Bradford Pals) waited for 'zero'. Beyond the valley floor the rest of the Durhams and 1st Bradford Pals and the entire 15/West Yorks (Leeds Pals) were waiting in the front and two support lines. Brigadier General John Darnley Ingles set up his 93 Brigade battle HQ 60m into the fields here.

Study the ground to the east. It is worth noting the distances that men were expected to travel from this point. The 12/KOYLI pioneers and 18/DLI towards the rear of the assembly area had to traverse some 750m to reach the British front line, a further 130m to the German front line and the final 93 Brigade objective was a full 2.5km further still – a total distance of almost 3.5km, much of it uphill and carrying up to 80lb in kit, equipment and extra supplies, including rolls of barbed wire, 5ft posts, boxes of staples, pliers, hammers and billhooks, on a day when the temperature reached 26 °C!

Continue and look left as you come in line with a clump of tall trees ❷. This is the Bois en Cuvette; **Basin Wood** on trench maps.

La Signy Farm – referred to as Ferme de Lassigny on modern maps – lies beyond. Now overgrown but once an almost circular depression, Basin Wood was set up as a regimental aid post and several men of the Pals battalions passed close by on 1 July. **Private Reg Parker** of the Sheffield City Battalion remembered seeing it 'full of wounded', lying around and groaning in the flash of the guns on the night of the attack, with three doctors 'working flat out'. The wounded **Corporal Albert Wood** of the 1st Bradford Pals managed to crawl half a mile back to this spot where he saw 'the most horrible sight'; his battalion medical officer, the Irishman **Captain Charles 'Paddy' Roche** RAMC, working at a trestle table in his vest with bodies 'piled like sandbags all around him'. His fellow surgeon in the 2nd Bradford Pals, Canadian **Captain George Boyd 'Mac' McTavish**, was one of the other doctors who toiled to the point of exhaustion. Both men were awarded the Military Cross for their 'conspicuous courage and skill' in tending the wounded here and in going out into no-man's-land later to rescue the wounded 'from points which were constantly under heavy fire'. McTavish, who went on to earn two bars to his MC, later wrote, 'I'll never forget July 1st as long as I live. It was an awful day.' He went on to serve in the Canadian RAMC in the Second World War and died in 1965.

Before going on it is worth remembering that those same slopes to your right were, at the beginning of June 1915, the site of the German front line which bulged out in a westerly salient towards you – the **Toutvent Farm** Salient (it became **'Touvent'** later). It was this salient that the French attacked on 7 June 1915 and in a bloody battle that lasted for seven days eight French regiments were thrown into the fight and doggedly drove the Germans back to the positions the British were to assault on 1 July 1916. French losses were 2,000 killed and 9,000 wounded and missing.

Continue to the junction of tracks marked by a line of concrete telegraph poles and look left towards la Signy Farm. In 1916 the cellars of the ruins were used as headquarters and observation posts. The 1908 Olympic gold medal rower, pianist and composer **Lieutenant Commander Frederick Septimus Kelly DSC** of the Hood Battalion of the Royal Naval Division brought his officers here on 10 October 1916 to study 'the lie of the land' shortly after The Hood had arrived on the Somme from the Souchez sector near Vimy Ridge.

You are now standing on the boundary that separated 93 from 94 Brigade – draw an imaginary line across the fields to your right bisecting the near 90-degree angle made by Sackville Street and the remains of what used to be a track to the right. A hundred years previously this was the main track through the woodland. There is no established track today but it is still possible to follow the edge of the field. Turn right passing another stand of tall trees – **Observation Wood** – ❸ after 350m. This feature is a very steep-sided circular depression and due to its elevated position and the protection it offered a trench nearby was used as the battle headquarters of Brigadier General Hubert Rees, who had recently assumed command of 94 Brigade. Look due east towards Sheffield Park to appreciate the view Brigadier General Rees had on the morning of 1 July 1916:

[The brigade major, Captain Francis] Piggott and I ... made our way to advanced brigade HQ in front of Observation Wood. HQ consisted of a steel shelter, with two exits, some 10 feet underground, capable of holding about 15 people. A similar shelter was provided ... for the signallers. A splendid view was obtainable from the trench outside over the whole of the ground as far as Serre. We were about 500 yards behind the front trench ... ten minutes before zero our guns opened an intense fire. I stood on top to watch. It was magnificent. The trenches in front of Serre changed shape and dissolved minute by minute under the terrific hail of steel. Watching, I began to believe in the possibility of a great success, but I reckoned without the Hun artillery. This ten minutes intense bombardment combined with the explosion of twenty tons of dynamite under the Hawthorn Redoubt near Beaumont Hamel must have convinced any enemy observer that the attack was in progress and, as our infantry advanced, down came a perfect wall of explosive along the front trenches of my brigade and the 93rd. It was the most frightful artillery display that I had seen up to that time and in some ways I think it was the heaviest barrage I have seen put down by the defence on any occasion.

As the German barrage increased in intensity Rees and his staff could only watch as the last assaulting waves of his Accrington, Barnsley and Sheffield Pals left their trenches near here and went into their first battle against a well-drilled and professional adversary:

I have never seen a finer display of individual and collective bravery than the advance of that brigade. I never saw a man waver from the exact line prescribed for him. Each line disappeared in the thick cloud of dust & smoke which rapidly blotted out the whole area. I can safely pay a tribute also to the bravery of the enemy, whom I saw standing up in their trenches to fire their rifles in a storm of fire. They actually ran a machine gun out into no man's land to help repel the attack. I saw a few groups of men through gaps in the smoke cloud, but I knew that no troops could hope to get through such a fire. My two staff officers, Piggott and Stirling, were considerably surprised when I stopped the advance of the rest of the machine gun company ... now passing my headquarters. It was their first experience of a great battle and all that morning they obviously found it difficult to believe that the whole brigade had been destroyed as a fighting unit.

With over optimistic and often contradictory messages pouring in, at 9.00am Rees was ordered to send in more men to support the attack, even though he was 'quite sure that we had not got anyone into Serre except a few prisoners'. Reluctantly, he ordered C and D companies of the 1st Barnsley Pals forward and observed that, 'One company was badly mauled' but he had seen enough and his actions from that moment undoubtedly saved lives:

I was ordered to send a company to bomb the Germans out of the front trench of the 93rd brigade [but] said that no front trenches existed, but to no purpose ... A little later I was talking to [OC 31st Division] General O'Gowan and told him that I didn't believe the Germans were in the 93rd's trench at all. He said, to my considerable astonishment, 'Nor do I'. 'In that case', said I 'I will stop the attack which you have just ordered me to make' and rushed out of the dug out to cancel the order.

Continue for another 380m, passing the site of **Staff Copse** – now ploughed over – on the left, to a T-junction of tracks. This is the point at which **Route 4** – which begins at Serre Road Cemetery No. 1 – merges with the current route and so the descriptions for both are now the same. Go straight on, passing the derelict brick building which marks the site of **Old Touvent Farm** ❹ on the left. The original farm was just behind the German front line in mid-1915, the farm giving its name to the German salient that the French 'flattened' in June that year.

Continue and pause after 230m. A major communication trench that marked the extreme left flank of the entire front to be attacked by the British Fourth Army on 1 July Somme crossed the track here. This was **Nairne Street** which ran for 1.4km from John Copse – the northern end of the belt of trees to your right – all the way back to a post called Fort Sussex. **Private Frank Lindley** of 14/York and Lancs (2nd Barnsley) was just 15 years old when he first came up Nairne Street in March 1916. The battalion had been in Egypt and was being issued with the Brodie steel helmet: 'We gave our pith helmets in at Nairne Street end, stuck a tin hat on, and up we went.' On 1 July Frank Lindley's A Company was in file in Nairne Street between this spot and John Copse. They were to go over with the first wave of the Sheffield City Battalion to capture and convert a German communication trench into a defensive line facing north to seal the northern flank of the entire Fourth Army advance: a critically important task for men who had been on the Western Front for just three months. Lindley remembers waiting in Nairne Street for zero somewhere off to your right. 'We were cheek by jowl … as we stood there one of their "coal boxes" [German 150mm shell emitting black smoke] dropped on the top … the next bloke to me started shaking – absolutely unhinged … I was next to Sergeant Jones and this salvo of shrapnel came right over … Some must have gone down the back of this sergeant … blood was coming out of his back'.

Continue towards the junction with the main road. You will cross the British front line just before hitting the road. ❺ New Touvent Farm, which you passed on the spine route, is to the left and Serre to the right. You have briefly crossed into the sector held by the 48th Division. There was to be no attack between here and the diversion at Gommecourt, only the release of smoke from the north to mask the 31st Division's attack.

Turn right and continue along the road – named **Serheb Road** – towards the buildings of Pierrard Farm ahead. Stop on the bend after 200m and look to the trees to your right. That is the site of what was John Copse and which now marks the northerly end of the narrow ribbon of woodland culminating in Sheffield Memorial Park. You are now looking down the length of no-man's-land clearly marked by the Crosses of Sacrifice of the three battlefield cemeteries of John Copse, Serre Road No. 3 and Queen's Cemetery. The German front-line fire trench crossed the road 75m further on.

After 450m take the track on the right next to an orchard ❻ which leads back towards the woodland. The second of the four lines – heavily wired here – that made up the German front-line system ran across the corner of the orchard ahead. You can see vestiges of it to your left. The front-line fire trench was 90m to the right.

As you come line abreast with the trees on your right, note that you are entering the left of 94 Brigade's sector around the 'copses'. Prior to 1914, there had been distinct clumps of trees – copses – on roughly the same footprint as the continuous stretch of woodland you see today. Starting with the trees nearest you and running north to south, these copses were named after three of the writers of the Gospels – John, Luke and Mark. A fourth copse – Matthew, of course – lay in the valley some 125m beyond the furthest tree on the left in the distance, and was ploughed over in 1982. By 1916 they had been blasted into stumps. This was the front allocated to 12/York and Lancs (Sheffield City) and 14/York and Lancs (2nd Barnsley Pals) on 1 July 1916. Their front line fringed the treeline for some 300m, roughly halfway along the wooded area, with 11/East Lancs (Accrington Pals) – with 13/York and Lancs (1st Barnsley) in support – stretching beyond for a similar distance. Imagine standing here on 1 July and see the men of C Company, Sheffield City Battalion advancing, right to left, up the slope towards Serre from their white 'alignment' tape, with A Company of the 2nd Barnsley Pals streaming from Nairne Street to join them. Lance Corporal Reg Glenn attached to battalion HQ – just beyond the trees – witnessed it:

> The whistles blew. They all stood up and started to move forward in a straight line. They hadn't gone but a few steps when they went down again. I thought they had been tripped by a wire across no man's land, but it soon became obvious why: we heard the machine guns chattering away ... Things got chaotic with the rest of the battalion trying to get forward. The wounded struggled to get back and John Copse soon became full of dead and wounded.

Frank Lindley was one of the first out of Nairne Street in the first wave on the extreme left flank here, 'almost touching' his platoon commander Second Lieutenant William Hirst. At Zero Hour Hirst – a month shy of his first wedding anniversary – blew his whistle and Frank heaved himself out of the trench to join the leading waves of 12/York and Lancs:

> We scrambled on to the fire step and then on the top. It wasn't long before [Hirst] got it ... a machine-gun bullet in the head but I only took a fleeting glance. We had orders to keep moving. I looked around. Our lads were all going on the right, there was nothing on the left. We had to go up [towards the German trenches]. It wasn't a steep rise, just undulating, but of course it seemed like a mountain that morning.

With German machine-gun, rifle and artillery fire scything through no-man's-land the leading waves withered away. Frank remembered the sight of:

> our lads ... going down in their waves; flop, flop, flop [the German] wire was bundled up in great rolls with just an odd gap

in between; perhaps two blokes could have got through at once but there wasn't a chance of that ... I remember the lads laid in rows, just as if they'd gone to sleep there, and the sun flashing on them bits of tin on their backs all down the lines. The machine guns just laid 'em out. Some were hanging on the wire, hanging like rags. Machine guns bullets were knocking 'em round as if it was washing hung on the line.

Frank Lindley never made it into the German trenches. The sheer volume of German fire rocked the British attack back on its heels and he found himself held up at the wire. Darting from shell hole to shell hole he was hit by a shell fragment which tore into his thigh. He could go no further. Miraculously, the – now – 16-year-old rolled back across no-man's-land in front of you and finally made it to the relative safety of the British front line where he was wounded again. Stretchered back, he was put on an ambulance and eventually reached Étaples where a doctor yanked the shell splinter out without anaesthetic. Frank then drifted into unconsciousness to the sound of someone sawing frantically! His platoon commander, William Hirst, is buried in Bertrancourt Military Cemetery (I.E.16), 7km west of the battlefield.

Continue along the track with the wooded copses on your right. The first cemetery you reach is **Luke Copse British Cemetery** ❼ which has a hedge-lined approach path leading down to a small rectangular cemetery with the headstones placed along the left-hand wall. The casualties were clearly buried in a former trench with the headstones in staggered pairs. Two of the casualties that morning were brothers, 25-year-old **Lance Corporal Frank Gunstone** (Grave 11) and his younger sibling, 24-year-old **Private William Gunstone** (Grave 21), who enlisted together in Sheffield. Another Sheffield soldier killed on 1 July was Barnsley-born 31-year-old **Private James Swift** (Grave 18), whose name can be found in the Sheffield Council Roll of Honour which is still displayed in Sheffield City Hall.

After leaving the cemetery turn right along the track towards **Queens Cemetery** ❽ which you can see in open fields in the former no-man's-land. It can be approached using the long grass path opposite the gate to the Sheffield Memorial Park but before visiting note that you have now crossed into the sector held by 11/East Lancs and 13/York and Lancs. At 7.20am the leading waves of W and X companies of the Accrington Pals under Captain Tough fixed bayonets and moved from the tree line through gaps in the British wire to a point about 50m to the left of this track under intense shell fire. There they lay down and waited for zero in what the men called 'the shilling seats', losing men all the time. Captain

Tough was wounded almost immediately. At 7.30am whistles blew and the Pals advanced up the slope, only to be torn apart – as the Sheffield and Barnsley men had – by deadly enfilade fire coming from behind you and where there had been no attack. You are now moving across ground that would have been strewn with dead and wounded Accrington and Barnsley men who had been in the second wave. Private Charles Taylor of 13/York and Lancs remembered that he:

> started crawling back towards our lines, and I had never seen so many dead men clumped together. That was all I could see and I thought to myself, 'All the world's dead – they're all dead – they're all dead.' That's all I could think as I crawled along. Everywhere I passed, to my left and right were dead men laying on the ground.

Walk up the grass track to Queen's Cemetery – originally known as Queen's V Corps Cemetery No. 4 – with its two distinctive conifers on either side of the Cross of Sacrifice. The 5 rows of headstones are positioned close together signifying that the 131 casualties are probably buried in a mass grave. One of two brothers who were killed on the Western Front, 26-year-old **Captain Arnold Tough** (11/East Lancs) (D.62) led the first wave into action from **Mark Copse** on 1 July. After qualifying as a dentist in 1911, he opened a practice on Avenue Parade, Accrington before accepting a commission into the Pals in September 1914. He was killed by a shot to the head. His brother, John, having qualified as a doctor of medicine, was commissioned into the RAMC in May 1917 and was killed serving with 5/Field Ambulance six weeks before the Armistice in 1918. Buried nearby is 41-year-old **Sergeant Harry Neill** (B.2) of 12/York and Lancs, whose death on 1 July prompted his parents to erect a plaque in St Helen's Church, Grindleford in Derbyshire where he was a lay reader. Here also lies **Captain Stewart Maleham** (C.34) who led two clearing platoons of A Company of the 1st Barnsley Pals behind the second wave of Accrington Pals.

Retrace your steps to the track and enter Sheffield Memorial Park through the gate opposite.

The preserved trenches, shell holes and collapsed dugouts you see today are part of the only stretch of the Somme battlefield preserved by the British; cared for by the CWGC and paid for by Sheffield City Council. Sheffield Memorial Park is, however, a misnomer, as it was the Accrington and Barnsley Pals who attacked from these trenches or came down the slopes of the valley opposite, to pass over this ground on their way into no-man's-land behind you. It is often repeated that the park

was instituted as a living memorial to the
Sheffield City Battalion alone but this is not
the case. The appeal to raise funds for what
was originally called the 'Sheffield-Serre
Memorial Park' was officially launched by the
Sheffield branch of the British War Graves
Association on 6 August 1927. The intention
was to 'secure for all time a Memorial Park
at Serre to all Sheffield men who fell during
the war in any theatre, whether in the air, on
land or at sea'. The sum of £800 was required
then to reimburse the expenses of the local
landowner – who lived in Calais and had
given the land freely – to compensate the
tenant farmer (£41.00 for loss of crops),

Captain Arnold Tough.

fence off the land and purchase costly insurance for workmen on
what was still an extremely dangerous 7-acre plot. Many sites could
have been considered but the trenches within the original boundary
of the park including – from north to south – parts of Nairne Street,
Jordan, Le Cateau and Excema communication trenches were chosen
as it was ground upon which the city's own battalion 'began and ended

The entrance to Sheffield Memorial Park shrouded in mist.

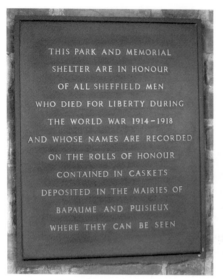

The plaque in the Memorial Shelter.

The park contains numerous memorials attached to the trees.

its history'. So the link with the Sheffield City Battalion was forged in the popular imagination although Sheffield had erected the battalion memorial in Serre village four years earlier.

The memorial pavilion you see halfway down the slope is not the first. The original – designed by architect F. Ratcliffe who had been a member of the City Battalion and was wounded on 1 July – was down the steps on the right. It was not simply an aesthetic addition, it had a very practical purpose and Sir Fabian Ware himself, vice president of what became the CWGC, took a keen interest in its construction. As the area had four cemeteries in close proximity but some distance from the roads it was felt that 'pilgrims' had need of a shelter in bad weather. The park and original shelter were officially opened on 25 May 1931 by J. Lawson MP, Parliamentary Secretary to the Ministry of Labour, representing Sir Fabian Ware, in front of a crowd of ten more MPs, the mayor of Puisieux, many ex-servicemen and parents of those killed. A Sheffield stainless steel casket containing a roll of honour bearing the names of all known – 4,898 – Sheffield men killed in the war was placed in the pavilion. Alderman John Graves told the assembled throng that they could now 'count this little plot of ground "Forever Sheffield"'. Unfortunately, the original shelter was battered by the weather and was replaced after the Second World War. As for the steel casket, that was hidden during the Second World War – along with some seventeen Allied airmen – by B. Leach, a War Graves Commission gardener, in various tool sheds of cemeteries within the area. It is now in the *Mairie* of Puisieux.

Follow the path downhill through the remnants of trenches and shell craters to find the path leading to **Railway Hollow Cemetery**. ❾ Taking its name from the former light railway that ran along the valley floor and situated in the former British support lines, this cemetery was begun by V Corps ambulance units in 1917 after the battlefield clearance. The 107 men of the 3rd, 19th and 31st divisions are buried in four rows, together with two French graves from the 1915 Toutvent Farm offensive: **Georges Palvadeau** and **Louis Lesourd**, were both killed on 7 June 1915. Hidden from the track opposite **Queens Cemetery** by the trees of Sheffield Memorial Park and suffering from occasional serious flooding, the cemetery contains the graves of forty-four identified men who were victims of the 1 July attack including twenty-three identified Sheffield City and 1st Barnsley Pals, fifteen Accrington Pals, two 1st Bradford Pals and two 12/KOYLI pioneers. One of these was 40-year-old **Company Sergeant Major William Loxley** (A.4) serving with B Company, Sheffield City Battalion. A former postman, Loxley was a South African War veteran who re-enlisted in October 1914. Having witnessed the destruction of the first wave of the attack, he was killed in the second wave. Another City Battalion sergeant is **Sergeant Maurice Charles Pilford Headeach MM** (B.4), husband of Charlotte Jemima Headeach, of Stokenchurch, High Wycombe and son of the Revd and Mrs Headeach. He had been Scout Master at Harrow for five years. A beautiful stained glass window is dedicated to his memory in St Peter and St Paul's, Stokenchurch. One of the memorable graves here is that of **Private Alfred Goodlad** of the Sheffield City Battalion (A.22) who was killed on 1 July and whose parents chose to use their son's own heartfelt words as his epitaph: 'The French are a grand nation. Worth fighting for. Vide Alf's letter 22.3.16.' Truly A Goodlad! There are also fifteen identified graves of Accrington Pals.

Retrace your route back to the park gate but before leaving follow the line of the shallow trench to the left to find a concrete cross. This was erected in memory of Albert Bull who was killed with the Sheffield City Battalion on 1 July 1916 and whose remains were found here during clearance work on the park in 1928. He was buried in Serre Road Cemetery No. 2, which we visit later.

Leave the park and turn right and follow the obvious track towards **Serre Road Cemetery No. 3** ❿ which you should be able to see ahead

Railway Hollow Cemetery.

of you. This track approximates the course of the British front line as you ascend the gentle slope and cross into the area of 93 Brigade 100m beyond the southern boundary of Sheffield Park. The German positions – a gentle bulge towards the British line on the crest of the rise 170m or so behind the cemetery – dominated the entire position here. The cemetery – containing seventeen Leeds and Bradford Pals – is situated in what was no-man's-land; the fields over the rear wall were the killing ground on which these and hundreds more of their comrades were cut down. There are eighty-one graves here, twenty-two of which are identified men who were killed on 1 July 1916 with a further four dying of wounds the next day. Commissioned in 1915, London-born 21-year-old Bradford Pal **Second Lieutenant Arthur Maitland** (Sp Mem 4) of 16/West Yorks was killed on 1 July and is the only identified officer in the cemetery. A former clerk with the Barnsley Traction Company, 20-year-old **Private Frank Bailey** (B.5) is the only Barnsley Pal killed on 1 July buried here. He enlisted in Barnsley in 1915. Spare a thought for 19-year-old Pudsey-born **Private Austin Thrippleton** (A.17) who was killed serving with 16/West Yorks and is one of at least nineteen Pudsey men who lost their lives on 1 July 1916.

Serre Road Cemetery No. 3 with the Cross of Sacrifice at Queens Cemetery visible in the distance.

From the cemetery re-join the track leading down to the farm on the D919 where a right turn will take you back to Serre Road Cemetery No. 1. As you descend reflect on the fact that the British front line did not follow the track but ran off diagonally to your right to pass behind the British and French cemeteries beyond the trees of the farm.

Looking towards the Cimetière National de Serre-Hébuterne from Serre Road Cemetery No. 2 with the Braithwaite Memorial visible to the left and the French Memorial Chapel to the right.

If you have left your vehicle at Serre Road Cemetery No. 2 a short walk along the D919 past the *Cimetière National de Serre-Hébuterne* will take you to your vehicle but as you pass the second of two entrances to the farm on the way, note that the original access route to Sheffield Park and the cemeteries around it ran through the farmyard here, up past Matthew Copse to Railway Hollow Cemetery.

Route 4

Serre – Alternative Start

A circular tour: around the Sheffield Memorial Park
Coordinates: 50°06′00.48″ N – 2°39′30.89″ E
Distance: 3.7km/2.3 miles
Suitable for: 🚶
Grade: Easy (total ascent 47m)
Maps: IGN Série Bleue 2407O – Acheux-en-Amiénois

General description and context: This is an alternative start to **Route 3** which avoids the walk along main D919 between Serre Road Cemetery Nos 1 and 2. This road can be extremely busy, particularly between September and January when it is used by sugar beet lorries. This short tour focuses on the 31st Division attack and joins **Route 3** just north of Railway Hollow Cemetery.

Directions to start: Park outside Serre Road Cemetery No. 1 **⑪** which you can approach along the D919 running between Mailly-Maillet and Puisieux.

Route description: Our route begins in what was no-man's-land with the British front line about 100m to your left. We suggest you leave your visit to Serre Road No. 1 and the French Chapel and National Cemetery until your return. With the cemetery on your left walk along the wide verge for approximately 80m until you see a track on your left and a cluster of CWGC signposts – one of which directs you to Sheffield Memorial Park. Walk up the track for 10m to find a memorial plaque to the men of **93 Brigade** who died on 1 July 1916. This is attached low down on the wall of a farm building to your left and, at the time of writing, was partly obscured by shrubs.

Continue uphill, along the track which now follows the British front line past the farm on the left. A few metres further on you meet another farm track on the left at the end of which you can see the rear of Serre Road Cemetery No. 1. As you walk over the rise **Serre Road Cemetery No. 3** comes into view **⑩** which we have described in **Route 3**. Almost opposite the cemetery gates the track forks. Take the left fork and descend into Railway Hollow, the woodland of Sheffield Memorial Park can be seen on the right. You are now behind the British front line. As the track descends into the shallow valley ahead Railway Hollow Cemetery ❾ comes into view on the right before the track rises again to meet the junction ahead. A glance across to the left will reveal the trees of Observation Wood ❷ on Sackville Street. At the junction turn right to join **Route 3**.

The memorial plaque to the men of 93 Brigade.

Serre Road Cemeteries Nos 1 and 2
Serre Road Cemetery No. 1 was begun in May 1917 and these original graves – mainly men of the 4th and 31st divisions who were killed on 1 July 1916 – can be found at the top of the cemetery in Plot I, Rows A to G. This is a large cemetery and as such we have concentrated on individuals who were killed during the 1 July attacks. Look out for 30-year-old **Private Arthur Axe** (I.A.12), a

Serre Road Cemetery No. 1.

noted musician who, for nine years prior to the war, was music master and organist at St John's College, Hurstpierpoint in Sussex. Enlisting at Colsterdale, he joined the Leeds Pals and was killed on 1 July advancing with 11 Platoon of 15/West Yorks. In the same battalion, 29-year-old Yorkshire country cricketer **Lieutenant Major William Booth** (Major was his given name) (I.G.14) was severely wounded advancing with the first wave and died in the arms of **Private Waddington** in a shell hole. Booth's sister never got over his death and kept a candle burning in his bedroom window in the hope that he would return. Named as one of Wisden's cricketers of the year in 1914, Booth played test cricket during the 1913–14 tour of South Africa whilst 'Abe' Waddington joined the Royal Flying Corps and survived the war to play in two test matches against Australia in 1920. Another Yorkshireman was 31-year-old **Second Lieutenant Robert Tolson** (I.B.52) who was killed fighting with A Company, 15/West Yorks. His brother, **Second Lieutenant James Tolson**, was killed on 20 October 1918, just days before the Armistice. Both boys have given their name to the Tolson Memorial Museum in Huddersfield. Commanding 1/King's Own in the 4th Division's attack on the *Heidenkopf* was 29-year-old **Major John Nisbet Bromilow** (I.B.51) who had already seen service and been a wounded in Gallipoli. He was initially posted as missing but his death is recorded as 2 July, six weeks after joining the battalion. Interestingly, **Lieutenant Victor Hawkins** of 2/Lancashire Fusiliers notes in his diary that Bromilow's body was not recovered until August 1917. **Second Lieutenant Brian Farrow** (I.C.6) had enlisted and served as a lance corporal in the Royal Fusiliers in 1914 before being commissioned in May 1915 and joining 2/Lancashire Fusiliers. He was killed – aged 24 – in no-man's-land on his way back from the *Heidenkopf* having fought there for most of the day. **Sergeant Frank Clayton** (I.C.38) was an accountant and in partnership with his brother William in Leeds. A Fellow of the Society of Accountants and Auditors and a member of the Headingley Lodge of Freemasons, he was also connected with the Leeds City Football club. Enlisting in September 1914, he was serving with A Company, 15/West Yorks when he was killed – aged 41– with most of 11 Platoon on 1 July. Finally, before you leave, find 29-year-old **Sergeant John Hall** (I.G.51) who was killed fighting with the 18/Durham Light Infantry just

Second Lieutenant Robert Tolson.

south of Matthew Copse. A shipyard plater before he enlisted in 1914, he was promoted to sergeant twelve months later in 1915. The remainder of the cemetery was added after the Armistice when casualties were brought in from the nearby battlefields and smaller cemeteries in the locality. There are now 2,426 casualties buried or commemorated here and of these over half are unidentified.

Serre Road Cemetery No. 2 is the largest British military cemetery on the Somme and was begun in May 1917. By 1918 it contained approximately 475 graves (Plots I and II, except for Row E, Plot II, which was added in 1922, and Row AA, Plot I, which was added in 1927). After the Armistice the cemetery was enlarged considerably by the addition of further graves from the surrounding area. Many of the original 1 July graves can be found behind the Stone of Remembrance, although others are scattered about the cemetery in clusters, presumably as they were found in outlying cemeteries and burial grounds. As we did with Serre Road Cemetery No. 1, we have concentrated our description on men who lost their lives on 1 July 1916. **Corporal James Allan** (I.G.39) of 2/Seaforth Highlanders was reported missing in action until his death was confirmed in August 1916. His brother, Private Morris Allan of 9/Gordon Highlanders, was killed at Loos on 25 September 1915. Hemstead-born **Private Charles Andrews** (I.J.2) of 2/Essex, enlisted in Saffron Walden and has his name inscribed on the Hemstead War Memorial. Buried close by is the architect and soldier-poet **Second**

Serre Road Cemetery No. 2.

Lieutenant Gilbert Waterhouse (I.K.23) also of 2/Essex who was commissioned in May 1915 and is one of twenty-two officer casualties sustained by the battalion during its attack on the *Heidenkopf*. His body was recovered and buried a year after the attack. A posthumous volume of his poetry – *Rail Head and Other Poems* – was published shortly after he went missing. Born in France, 20-year-old **Private Horace Bearley** (I.J.23) was one of the first men to enter the *Heidenkopf* trenches with 1/8 Royal Warwicks. His name is also to be found in the Birmingham City Hall of Memory. Educated at Marlborough College, 22-year-old **Second Lieutenant Henry Field** (II.C.10) was commissioned into the Royal Warwickshire Regiment in September 1914 and joined 1/6 Royal Warwicks in February 1916 at Foncquevillers. During his training he wrote 'A Carol for Christmas 1914' but left the last line unfinished. **Private Thomas Cooper** (I.K.30) was 26 years old when he was killed fighting with C Company, 1/8 Royal Warwicks. Prior to his enlistment he lived in Knowle near Solihull with his Aunt Mary and worked as a farm labourer.

Brought into the cemetery later was **Captain Stratford Ludlow** (XXXIX.E.12) who was killed with 1/8 Royal Warwicks and may well have known Thomas Cooper who served in the same company. Ludlow's grave is to the right of the Stone of Remembrance, as is that of **Private John Chapman** (XXXIX.J.11.) of 14/York and Lancs (2nd Barnsley Pals) who was born in Gawber and enlisted in Barnsley. He was one of the 550 casualties recorded by the battalion on 1 July. Amongst the many other casualties of 1 July brought into the cemetery after 1917 were numerous men of the Royal Irish Rifles who fought with the 36th Division at Thiepval. **Captain James Davidson** (XXX.E.7), who was attached to 108 Brigade Machine Gun Company from 13/Royal Irish Rifles, was shot dead as he was being assisted back to the British lines. Located to the left of the Cross of Sacrifice is 38-year-old **Sergeant Fred Guntley** (XIII.D.5) of 15/Royal Irish Rifles who married Rachel in 1908 in Belfast but was living in London at the outbreak of war. Before you leave find 22-year-old **Private Albert Bull** (XIX.E.16) whose grave is close to the Cross of Sacrifice. He was killed with the 12/York and Lancs but his body was not found for many years and he has a private memorial to his memory – visited earlier – in Sheffield Memorial Park.

The French National Cemetery and Memorial Chapel

You will find the *Cimetière National de Serre-Hébuterne* adjacent to Serre Road Cemetery No. 1 and, on the other side of the road, a small memorial chapel which was built in 1936. Many of the men buried in the French cemetery took part on the attack on **Old Toutvent Farm**

The Cimetière National de Serre-Hébuterne.

between 7 and 13 June 1915. Ten years later, in June 1925, a memorial to the French 56th Division was erected in the cemetery and on the steps leading up to the **French Memorial Chapel** you will find a plaque honouring the dead of the four French divisions that took part in the assault. On the left of the chapel porch is another plaque to the memory of **Maître Joseph de la Rue**, who was chaplain to both the 243rd and 233rd Infantry Regiments during the June 1915 attack and is said to have been instrumental in the construction of the French National

The French Memorial Chapel.

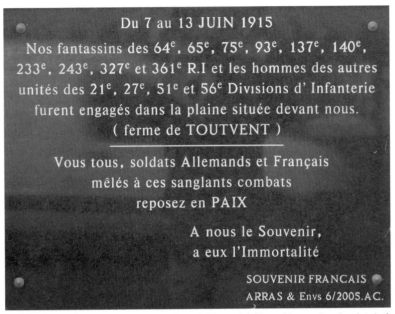

Du 7 au 13 JUIN 1915

Nos fantassins des 64ᵉ, 65ᵉ, 75ᵉ, 93ᵉ, 137ᵉ, 140ᵉ, 233ᵉ, 243ᵉ, 327ᵉ et 361ᵉ R.I et les hommes des autres unités des 21ᵉ, 27ᵉ, 51ᵉ et 56ᵉ Divisions d' Infanterie furent engagés dans la plaine située devant nous.
(ferme de TOUTVENT)

Vous tous, soldats Allemands et Français mêlés à ces sanglants combats reposez en PAIX

A nous le Souvenir, a eux l'Immortalité

SOUVENIR FRANCAIS
ARRAS & Envs 6/2005.AC.

The plaque near the entrance to the French Memorial Chapel honouring the dead of the four French divisions that took part in the assault on Old Touvent Farm.

Cemetery. On the left by the entry porch is a rare German memorial plaque erected in 1964 in memory of BRIR 1, which garrisoned the German line at Serre in 1917 in the most appalling weather conditions which were made considerably worse by accurate British shell fire. After returning to your vehicle you may wish to make the short journey to visit **Sucrerie Military Cemetery**.

To find Sucrerie Military Cemetery keep Serre Road Cemetery No. 2 on your left and follow the D919 for 1.7km to the crossroads with the D174. The cemetery will be seen to your right front marked by a clump of trees. Continue over the crossroads and take the next track on the right. The former sugar beet factory which gave the cemetery its name was on the right of the track just before the bend. Parking can be difficult and it may be advisable to park safely after the crossroads and approach the cemetery on foot.

Sucrerie Military Cemetery was begun in 1915 by the French and extended by British units until December 1918. It was first called the 10th Brigade Cemetery and was one of the principal routes British

Sucrerie Military Cemetery.

troops took from the village of Colincamps towards the front line. The 285 French and 12 German graves were removed to other cemeteries after the Armistice, and in consequence there are gaps in the lettering of the rows. There are now 1,103 casualties buried here and of these 219 casualties are unidentified, a number of which are buried in the far right-hand corner of the cemetery where a cluster of 7 headstones near the Stone of Remembrance mark the graves of 24 unidentified soldiers.

Of the 155 officers and men who were killed on 1 July or died of wounds the following day are 25 officers and men of 1/King's Own. Their costly assault on the *Heidenkopf* in support of the Warwicks and The Rifle Brigade – an assault that should never have gone in – left twenty-three officers killed or wounded. Lieutenant Victor Hawkins of 2/Lancashire Fusiliers was at 12 Brigade HQ that morning:

Just before the brigade went over the division wired us to stop the battalions and also stop the 10th Brigade. Runners were immediately sent to the King's Own and Essex, Lan Fus, Dukes. They were too late however. The King's Own and Essex were right on. The Lan Fus were mostly in the Quadrilateral and one coy of the Dukes was in the Bosch line. The result of all this was that the

93rd Brigade having failed on the left and the 29th Division on the right, the German came down from either flank and the King's Own and Essex were practically missing. Major Bromilow has not been heard of since … Col Stirling, the CO Essex, was wounded twice at the beginning and got away. [Captain Lawrence] Cadic, the adjutant of the Essex, and the adjutant of the King's Own were both wounded. Fighting went on all afternoon. Some of the Seaforths of the 10th Brigade got over and joined up with the Lan Fus in the quadrilateral. The CO of the Seaforths, Hodge, Bertie Ravenscroft, Hall, Watkins, Mansell and Rougier in the 'Quad' with him and stayed there till 2.00am July 2nd bombing the whole time. CSM Laverick and Sgt Albon were in there too. These two found a Stokes gun and although they had never seen one before worked it till they ran dry of ammunition. [Brian] Farrow [see Serre Road Cemetery No. 1] was killed in no man's land on his way back having been with the others all the time. The Roman Road on the afternoon of July 1st was ghastly, wounded in every place conceivable coming up all the time. Macdonald with a bullet in his chest and a Bosch helmet was the only one of the officers I saw from the Regt. He was quite happy … The sum total of the attack was a bad hammering and no ground captured, but from all accounts Bosch lost heavily too.

Second Lieutenant Hugh Melly (I.H.11), who joined the King's Own from the 3rd Battalion Liverpool Regiment after leaving Malvern College in 1914, lies here. Wounded in 1915, he returned to the Somme shortly before 1 July. Commissioned in December 1915 and from Heywood in Lancashire, 21-year-old **Second Lieutenant Percy Clegg** (I.H.3) was one of only four officers of the King's Own whose bodies were recovered from the battlefield.

Second Lieutenant Hugh Melly.

Educated at Eton, 45-year-old **Lieutenant Colonel Hon. Lawrence Palk** DSO (I.H.14) was killed along with 26 officers and 559 men whilst commanding 1/Hampshires south of **Ridge Redoubt** on the Redan Ridge. He was the son of the 2nd Baron Haldon and is said to have led his battalion over no-man's-land wearing white gloves and wielding a cane. Mortally wounded, he is reported to have turned to another man lying next to him and said, 'If you know of a better 'ole, go to it.' Nearby is **Lieutenant Colonel**

John Thicknesse (I.H.75) who was killed commanding the 1/Somerset Light Infantry along with his adjutant **Captain Charles Ford** (I.I.67) who died of wounds on 2 July. Thicknesse had previously served in the South African War and on the North-West Frontier and was the son of the Revd Francis Thicknesse, the late Bishop of Leicester. Another 1/Somersets soldier was 21-year-old **Private Bertie Chant** (I.D.26) from Yeovil, whose headstone is inscribed with the words 'Never Forgotten by his Loving Mother and Father', an epitaph that could be emblazoned across almost every grave in the cemetery. Before you leave spare a thought for **Private James Crozier** (I.A.5) of 9/Royal Irish Rifles who was executed for desertion in February 1916 and originally buried in the grounds of the chateau at Mailly-Maillet before his remains were moved here.

Serre Road Cemetery No. 1 to Beaumont Hamel

Distance: 2.6km/1.6 miles
Suitable for: 🚗 ⛽

Immediately across the road from **Serre Road Cemetery No. 1** is a minor road with a CWGC signpost directing you to the three Redan Ridge Cemeteries, Waggon Road Cemetery and Munich Trench Cemetery. Take this road and continue uphill. Named **Frontier Lane** by the British, this road ran a little way behind and parallel to the German second-line trenches. You are now ascending the **Redan Ridge**, one of the areas often ignored by the battlefield tourist. It was the most northerly sector of the British front line where large-scale tunnelling activity was still being carried out in July 1916. On 1 July the sector was assaulted by the regular troops of the 4th Division with two Territorial battalions – 1/6 and 1/8 Warwicks – from the 48th Division attached for the attack.

Continue for 400m or so until you can look back for good views of the French Memorial Chapel, the French National Cemetery and Serre Road Cemetery No. 1. You are now behind the site of the *Heidenkopf* which we look at in **Route 3.** The British front line lay across the main D919 road some 250–300m to your right. The ground around you here was the scene of fierce fighting during the afternoon and evening of 1 July whilst the slope beyond the road opposite was a scene of utter carnage as the follow-up battalions of 11 and 93 Brigades came under deadly enfilade fire from **Ridge Redoubt**, some 650m on the crest up ahead as they attempted to follow the assaulting waves. Ahead of you, on the right, is the end wall of Serre Road Cemetery No. 2.

Brigadier General Charles Bertie Prowse, commanding 11 Brigade, was mortally wounded by machine-gun fire from the area of Ridge Redoubt as he moved his brigade HQ forward into the German front line in the *Heidenkopf* in the mistaken belief that it had been secured. Prowse – who had risen from the rank of major in August 1914 to brigadier general by April 1915 – had been Val Braithwaite's commanding officer when the latter earned his MC near Ploegsteert Wood in late 1914 and today has a cemetery – Prowse Point – named after him near the spot where that action occurred. Four commanding officers of the six battalions under Prowse's command on 1 July were killed during the attack, whilst 41-year-old **Major Lionel Walsh,** commanding 2/Royal Dublin Fusiliers in 10 Brigade, died of wounds three days later at 4 Casualty Clearing Station in Beauval, 6km south of Doullens. He is buried in Beauval Communal Cemetery. His sister, Beatrice Scott-Smith, who lived at Banks Hall in Cawthorne near Barnsley, placed a tablet in his memory in All Saints' church in the village.

On the right flank the 1/East Lancashires were particularly hard hit by machine-gun fire, losing 502 officers and men killed and wounded, including **Lieutenant Colonel James Green** who eventually got back to his lines at 8.30pm.

Continue along the road until you reach a calvary on the right together with a CWGC signpost for Redan Ridge Cemeteries Nos 3 and 1. Park where convenient. The track on the right leads to the entrance to **Redan Ridge Cemetery No. 3**, which was just inside the German front line. The high ground above the cemetery is the approximate site of what the British named **Ridge Redoubt** but which was not really a strongpoint at all, merely a small salient resulting from mining activity in late 1914 as the French and Germans tussled for the 140m contour at the crest. The Germans referred to it variously as the *Minenfeld Beaumont* or the *Sodenbogen*. It was in the German third-line trenches somewhere just north of this spot that around midday on 1 July someone gave the order to retire and there was immediate panic amongst the largely leaderless and intermingled remnants of the battalions of 11 Brigade. Some got up and tried to run back to the British lines but as soon as they exposed themselves they were cut down. In an attempt to restore discipline, **Lieutenant Colonel John Hopkinson**, the commanding officer of 2/Seaforth Highlanders in 10 Brigade, ordered **Drummer Walter Ritchie** to stop the flight by sounding the 'Charge' on his bugle. The Seaforths' adjutant, **Captain John Laurie**, recalled watching Ritchie, one of his HQ orderlies, jump up from his shell hole in the face of enemy fire and blow his bugle constantly. 'This had the desired effect and stopped the rot.' For this action and for repeatedly carrying messages under fire that day, Drummer Ritchie was awarded the **Victoria Cross**, which he received from King George V at Buckingham Palace on 25 November 1916. Ritchie survived the war and died in Edinburgh in 1965. The ridge was not finally captured until November 1916 when the German front line was pushed back to **Waggon Road** by the 2nd Division.

Take the track to Redan Ridge Cemetery No. 3. This is a small cemetery containing over sixty-seven casualties of which over half are unidentified. On either side of the entrance are thirteen graves that were destroyed by shell fire, now represented by special memorials. The great majority of the officers and men buried here fell in November 1916 and belonged to the 2nd Division, although there is one identified casualty of 1 July, 22-year-old **Lance Corporal Frederick Purdue** (B.6) from Basingstoke who was killed with 1/Hampshires during their attack south of Ridge Redoubt.

Leave the cemetery and turn right along the track for 250m until **Redan Ridge Cemetery No. 1** comes into view. Access is via the grass pathway. Situated in no-man's-land the cemetery was made by V Corps ambulance units in the spring of 1917 when the battlefields were cleared. Of the 154 graves 44 are casualties of the 1 July fighting and

Drummer Walter Ritchie VC.

largely from 11 and 12 Brigades. **Second Lieutenant Aubrey Holmes** (A.50) enlisted in 1914 and was commissioned from the ranks in May 1915 into 2/Essex and was one of the twenty-two officer casualties suffered by the battalion that day. In the next grave is 34-year-old **Second Lieutenant Henry Whitgreave** (A.51) who was killed fighting with 1/Somersets in the area of the *Heidenkopf*. Before you leave, find the grave of 26-year-old **Rifleman Henry Canepe** (A.28) from Highgate, London. He enlisted in May 1915 and arrived in France on 15 June 1916. He was killed serving with 1/Rifle Brigade less than three weeks later on 1 July.

Leave the cemetery and retrace your steps to the calvary. As you descend the track you should be able to see two CWGC cemeteries on the far side of the valley on **Waggon Road** ahead of you. On the left is **Munich Trench British Cemetery** and on the right is **Frankfurt Trench British Cemetery**, both of which are accessible from Beaumont Hamel.

At the calvary turn right towards Beaumont Hamel passing a track on the right marked by a CWGC signpost for **Redan Ridge Cemetery**

No. 2 – which we will be visiting in **Route 5**. Continue downhill and after another 150m you will cross the divisional boundary between the 4th and 29th divisions. Where the road meets the D163 you will find the 51st Highland Division flagpole commemorating the capture of the village by units of the 51st Highland Division on 13 November 1916. Reinstated by the Scottish Branch of the Western Front Association, it was unveiled on the ninetieth anniversary of the battle in 2006. A new plaque by the flagpole provides information about the attack on 13 November, along with a verse written by the poet 24-year-old **Lieutenant Ewart Mackintosh MC** of 1/5 Seaforth Highlanders, who died in November 1917. Turn left then immediately right and park near the church.

Lieutenant Ewart Mackintosh MC.

Route 5

Beaumont Hamel

A circular tour beginning at: Beaumont Hamel church
Coordinates: 50°05′01.90″ N – 2°39′23.09″ E
Distance: 6.5km/4.0 miles
Suitable for: 🚶 🚲
Grade: Easy (total ascent 90m)
Toilets: Newfoundland Park Visitor Centre
Maps: IGN Série Bleue 2407O – Acheux-en-Amiénois

General description and context: Beaumont Hamel was behind German lines until 13 November 1915 when units of the 51st Highland Division took the village in the closing stages of the Battle of the Somme. Adopted by Winchester after the war, the British attack in and around the village on 1 July 1916 was undertaken by the 29th Division which, under the command of **Major General Henry de Beauvoir Lisle,** had only arrived on the Western Front from Gallipoli in March 1916. Beaumont Hamel was a fortress in miniature, defended by RIR 119 and protected by the Redan and Hawthorn ridges. The British decision to fire a huge mine under the Hawthorn Redoubt at 7.20am – a full 10 minutes before zero– was clearly a mistake, as was the decision to lift the artillery barrage from the German front line at the same moment! Alerted by the blast of the mine the German defenders quickly manned their front lines from the relative safety of their deep dugouts and began to pour a withering fire on the attacking waves. The 86 Brigade attack was over almost before it had begun. Unable to occupy the far lip of the deep Hawthorn mine crater, 2/Royal Fusiliers were forced to withdraw by midday. The 1/Lancashire Fusiliers and 16/Middlesex – attacking north and south of the present-day D163 – came under a devastating fire from Beaumont Hamel and Hawthorn Ridge and were cut down long before reaching the German lines, a story that was repeated south of the Hawthorn mine crater where 2/Royal Dublin Fusiliers also lost heavily with 14 officers and 311 men becoming casualties.

Further to the south, in the 87 Brigade sector, 2/South Wales Borderers were cut down before they had advanced a few metres from their trenches by a combination of fire from machine guns sited in the

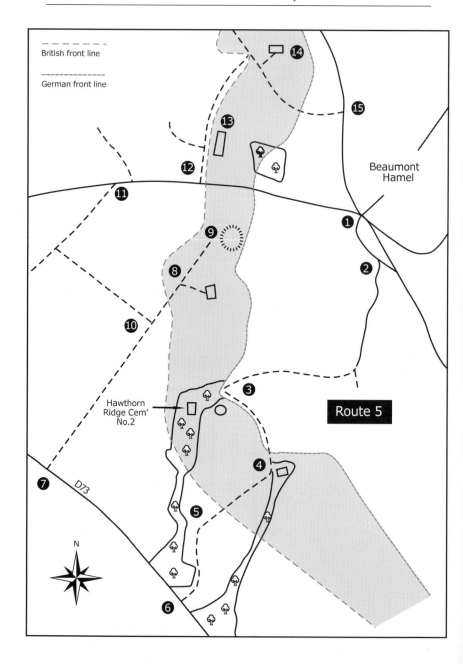

slightly more elevated rear banks of a natural cleft called Y Ravine and those further behind on the high ground of the Beaucourt Spur. To their right 1/Royal Inniskilling Fusiliers gained a foothold in the German first line north of the small British salient called Mary Redan, before they too were shot down. Unfortunately, a misunderstanding failed to prevent 1/Border Regiment and 1/King's Own Scottish Borderers from making their attack which was eventually brought to a bloody halt minutes later. Delays in communicating this disaster prompted de Lisle to order up his supporting brigade. The 1/Essex soon became bogged down with the dead and dying in the forward trenches, a scenario that also faced **Lieutenant Colonel Arthur Hadow** and

Lieutenant Colonel Arthur Hadow.

1/Newfoundland Regiment. Forced to leave the comparative safety of the communication trenches, they began their advance in full view of the German machine-gunners. Incredibly, a handful managed to make it to the German wire but their losses were staggering. Only 68 men were present when roll call was taken next morning – 684 officers and men had been killed, wounded or were missing believed killed. Only one other battalion suffered heavier casualties that day – 10/West Yorks at Fricourt (see **Route 9**). The 29th Division attack had effectively been crushed and with the single exception of the British break in at the *Heidenkopf* the German line was intact from south of Beaumont Hamel to Serre within an hour of the British attack being launched.

Directions to start: Beaumont Hamel is situated on the D163 between Auchonvillers and Beaucourt-sur-l'Ancre. Parking is available in the Place de l'Eglise by the church.

Route description: The church ❶ was rebuilt in 1922 and all that remains of the old church is a single pane of stained glass depicting the head of the Virgin Mary, which was returned in 1978 by a former German officer who picked it up as a souvenir during his time in the village. You will find this to the left of the entrance. With the church behind you turn right and then first left along the Rue Favrel and continue downhill until you see the village war memorial on your right. Directly opposite is a CWGC signpost directing you to the 51st Highland Division Memorial. Turn right here ❷ and follow the Rue du Parc uphill past farm buildings on your left. As you continue uphill note the steep bank on the right, in which the entrances to numerous German dugouts would have been located.

Continue to where the track branches off to the right, noting the line of trees almost directly ahead of you marking the position of **Y Ravine** – known to the Germans as *Leiling Schlucht*. Bear right and as you approach the northern entrance ❸ to **Newfoundland Memorial Park** the track runs almost parallel to Y Ravine. Before you pass through the barrier, glance across to your right to see the large clump of trees marking the site of the Hawthorn Crater, which we will visit later. Cycling is not allowed in **Newfoundland Memorial Park** so before entering remember to dismount if you are completing the tour by bike. This is a good time to look left into Y Ravine which, even today, is of considerable depth – up to 10m in places – but is now fenced off to prevent access. Honeycombed with deep dugouts, it was key to the German defence of this sector and a formidable physical obstacle in its own right. **Lieutenant Norman Collins** of 6/Seaforth Highlanders was able to examine Y Ravine after the successful 51st Highland Division attack on Beaumont Hamel on 13 November 1916: 'The dugouts themselves were very deep and had a flight of stairs down to the bottom and wire beds. There was even a system of brass bells, like

Y Ravine. Note the two figures on the right emphasizing the size of the ravine.

you would see in a house, which a batman could ring before entry into the innermost rooms.'

Take the track on the right to the circular **Hunter's Cemetery** and turn around to face the way you have come. Running off half left are the preserved trenches that formed the snout of the German front line around Y Ravine. The **51st Highland Division Memorial** to your right stands immediately behind the German front line, which then continues to snake off and pass behind **Y Ravine Cemetery** before jinking southeast eventually to run downhill into the Ancre valley. Behind you, the course of the British fire trench is 50–60m in front of the line of conifers on the western edge of the park. You are standing on one of the few places on the Somme battlefields where the German line is below that of the British.

Continue to **Hawthorn Ridge No. 2 Cemetery** which was begun by V corps in 1917. There are now 214 casualties commemorated here of which over 50 are unidentified. This is in reality a 29th Division cemetery containing men who were killed on 1 July during the attacks on the Hawthorn Crater and Y Ravine. **Second Lieutenant John Baxendine** (B.42) was gazetted to 1/Border Regiment in April 1915 and served in Gallipoli, taking part in the Suvla Bay landings. Invalided home, he subsequently served in Egypt and France. He was 22 years old when he died on 1 July. His younger brother, Richard Baxendine, served in Salonika but tragically died of pneumonia shortly after the Armistice in December 1918. John Baxendine may well have known **Second Lieutenant Arthur Frazer** DSO (A.33) who was seventeen years his senior and was last seen on the German wire encouraging his company forward. **Lieutenant Allan Haycraft** (B.44), who arrived on the Western Front in May 1916, was another relatively elderly subaltern who was killed, aged 32, serving with 2/Royal Fusiliers. Another Royal Fusiliers officer was 22-year-old **Second Lieutenant Leslie Westaway** (B.98) who was killed on Hawthorn Ridge. A former member of London University OTC, he was originally posted as missing until his death was confirmed twelve months later. **Second Lieutenant Robert Wallace Ross** (A.51) of 1/Newfoundland Regiment was 22 years old when he died and may well have been one of the myriad of corpses recovered by Norman Collins and his burial party in late November 1916. Collins described the dead Newfoundlanders who had been killed on 1 July as: 'Looking very ragged and the rats were running out of their chests. The rats were getting out of the rain of course, because the cloth over the rib cage made quite a nice nest … However when you touched a body the rats just poured out of the front.' During this period the remains of 669 men were collected from the surrounding 1 July battlefields and buried. The body of 21-year-old **Private Reginald Paul** (A.8) was another Newfoundlander whose body had remained where it had fallen on 1 July. Born in Burin, Newfoundland, he enlisted into the regiment in December 1914 and served in Gallipoli before arriving on the Somme. He left behind his wife Amelia and a young daughter, Dorothy.

Retrace your steps to **Hunter's Cemetery** where forty-six soldiers of the 51st Highland Division, who fell in the capture of Beaumont Hamel, were buried after the battle in a shell hole. Norman Collins and his burial party were possibly responsible for their burial as he writes of 'shovelling the dead into shell holes'. There are no 1 July casualties buried here. From the cemetery continue along the marked grass path which leads behind the **51st Highland Division Memorial**. Walk down the steps of the memorial to view the sculpture of the magnificent kilted highlander – modelled on **CSM Bob Rowan** of the Glasgow Highlanders and fashioned by sculptor George Paulin of Clackmannanshire – who faces the village the Jocks captured on 13 November 1916. On the front of the Rubislaw granite base is a plaque inscribed in Gaelic: *La a'Blair s'math n Cairdean*, the English translation of which is 'Friends are good on the day of battle'. The memorial was first unveiled by Ferdinand Foch in September 1924 and re-dedicated in July 1958 when those of the

Hunter's Cemetery with the 51st Highland Division Memorial in the background.

division who fell in the Second World War were commemorated. Now walk across to the wooden cross directly opposite, which is dedicated to the officers, NCOs and men of the 51st Highland Division who fell at High Wood near Longueval during their two attacks there in late July 1916.

From the memorial walk towards Y Ravine Cemetery ❹ along the metalled track. You are still behind the German front line here and will shortly see a numeric marker – Point 5 – at ground level indicating the former site of a tunnel entrance that led to dugouts on the far side of Y Ravine. Continue until you reach the next marker – Point 4 – and stop. This is where the German front line crossed the track and headed off towards the Ancre valley. On the right at the top of the park the striking bronze **Caribou Monument** – specific to commemorating five sites of significance to Newfoundland on the Western Front – can be seen braying mournfully across the battlefield for her fallen sons. Across to your far left is the Beaucourt Spur where the machine guns, which inflicted so many casualties on the battalions attacking across the ground between you and the caribou, were situated in the German main second-line defences.

The 51st Highland Division Memorial.

Continue to **Y Ravine Cemetery** where over 400 men are buried. These burials are mainly casualties of 1 July and 13 November but sadly over a third are unidentified. After having served at Gallipoli in 1915, 27-year-old **CSM Joseph Fairbrass** of 2/South Wales Borderers (C.66) was killed here on 1 July. Two of his five brothers were also killed during the war: William in April 1917 and Walter, who died on HMS *Pembroke* in November 1918. **Private Richard**

The 51st Division High Wood Memorial.

Maddigan (C.1) of 1/Newfoundland Regiment shares a headstone with **Private Isaac Moss** of 2/South Wales Borderers: both men were

Y Ravine Cemetery.

killed on 1 July and both were the same age, 19. Moss was a former coal miner and Maddigan an office clerk in St John's, Newfoundland and although the two boys had never met, it was only recently that the two families, on opposite sides of the Atlantic, finally made contact. **Lieutenant Richard Shortall** (C.44) enlisted in September 1914 and was commissioned in April 1915. The former engineer with the Reid-Newfoundland Company, which operated the Newfoundland Railway across the island, was wounded at Suvla in Gallipoli whilst serving with A Company, 1/Newfoundland Regiment. After re-joining the battalion at Suez in March 1916 he was killed on 1 July. Note that the emblem of the Newfoundland Regiment is the caribou rather than the maple leaf as Newfoundland did not become part of the Canadian Confederation until 1949.

Just before you leave the cemetery, pause by the entrance. There is a tendency on the part of many visitors – entirely understandable given the lie of the land and post-war layout of the park, exacerbated by the mature trees and the profusion of trenches and pathways – to become disorientated as to the direction of the British attack on 1 July. The axis of the attack did not follow the trend of a line running from the Caribou Monument towards the German line behind the 51st Highland Division Memorial, but from the caribou towards Y Ravine Cemetery where you are now standing.

Now look almost straight ahead and you should be able to see a small, isolated clump of living trees next to the petrified stump of the so-called '**Danger Tree'**, which is our next stop. Follow the track uphill to pass over Wellington Trench – Point 3 – which was dug after the battle of 1 July and used by the troops of the 51st Division during their attack on 13 November 1916. Stop by the Danger Tree. You are in the middle of no-man's-land now and at the spot where the Newfoundlanders' gallant advance effectively ground to a halt at 9.45am amidst a barrage of shrapnel and machine-gun fire – although a few did manage to get to the German wire where they were either killed or wounded. The shallow depression to the right of the track below the bank on which the original solitary battle-scarred tree stood was one of few precious patches of 'dead ground' on this sector and drew men, both wounded and unwounded, who had made it thus far seeking cover from the unremitting fire like a magnet. Although out of sight the lone tree – and note that from photographs taken in 1919 the original tree was very different in shape and size from the relic you see here today – it was indeed a place of 'danger'; the lynchet on which the original tree stood stretched all the way to the edge of the park and could be registered by German artillery. Those men who gathered around the tree and were

The Danger Tree.

lying wounded in shell holes elsewhere on the battlefield had to endure many hours under the July sun until darkness allowed a means of escape. Even then the journey was hazardous in the extreme. Imagine now **Private James McGrath**, who later told the *Newfoundland Quarterly* that the Germans 'mowed us down like sheep', crawling painfully back across the ground here from the area near Y Ravine Cemetery towards the vicinity of the caribou as you read his story:

> I managed to get to their barbed wire, where I got the first shot; then went to jump into their trench when I got the second in the leg. I lay in no-man's-land for fifteen hours, and then crawled a distance of a mile and a quarter. They fired on me again, this time fetching me in the left leg, and so I waited for another hour and moved again, only having the use of my left arm now. As I was doing splendidly, nearing our own trench they again fetched me, this time around the hip as I crawled on. I managed to get to our own line which I saw was evacuated as our artillery was playing heavily on their trenches. They retaliated and kept me in a hole for another hour. I was then rescued by Captain Windeler who took me on his back to the dressing station a distance of two miles.

Continue to cross over the British front line at Point 2 a little further on. The front line at this point was constructed on the forward slope and there are still some metal screw pickets as evidence of the sweep of the British wire. Continue along the marked grass pathway towards the **Caribou Monument ❺** – designed by British sculptor Basil Gotto – and climb to the top which allows you a good view of the entire battlefield and the British line of advance. Below the monument is the **Newfoundland Memorial to the Missing**, 3 brass panels bearing the names of over 800 officers and men of Newfoundland forces who lost their lives on land and at sea and who have no known grave.

The Newfoundlanders were in the second wave of the British attack and were tasked to pass through 2/South Wales Borderers and 1/Border Regiment. However, with the failure of both these battalions to take the German line the Newfoundlanders and 1/Essex were ordered to advance, although in the event, the Newfoundlanders attacked much earlier, independently of the Essex. Even before they reached no-man's-land they had to cross the British front-line trenches to get through the wire and as soon as the battalion crossed the brow of the ridge – approximately where the line of conifers on your left is today – they came under machine-gun fire which cut many of them down before their advance across no-man's-land began. In 1921 **Major**

The Caribou Memorial is one of five to be found on the Western Front.

Arthur Raley recalled that 'the only visible sign that the men knew they were under this terrific fire was that they all instinctively tucked their chins into an advanced shoulder as they had so often done when fighting their way home against a blizzard in some little outport in far off Newfoundland'.

Private Charlie 'Ginger' Byrne of 2/Hampshires was attached to the Newfoundlanders as part of a machine-gun team:

> I didn't go over the top with dash as you might say – more of a humping and a scrambling really. No yelling 'Charge' or anything like that. I kept my eye on the officer just ahead. He turned to wave us fellers on and then down he went – just as though he was bloody pole-axed. I just kept moving. I wasn't thinking really straight. My job was to keep with the gun-team. 'Don't lose me,' the Number One had said. So I kept on.

The 1/Essex advance had become bogged down amongst the dead and wounded in the forward trenches and progress was practically impossible, the same circumstances forced the Newfoundlanders to leave the security of the communication trenches and, with no supporting infantry and very little artillery, to move forward at ground level into a maelstrom of German gun fire. Ginger Byrne recalled that as he went over'there was blokes laying everywhere … the troops trying to advance had to jump over them … I could see near four hundred yards ahead and to my right … and there wasn't a man upright in the middle of no man's land. And yet these poor old Newfoundlanders went on. You had to admire them.'

You have just walked in the opposite direction from that taken by the Newfoundlanders towards the German front-line trenches behind you, a line also taken by **Private Arthur Osmond** in his attempt to reach the German trenches:

> Within a couple of hundred yards from the German lines I got a bullet through my right lung and I thought I was up. I was a bomber at that time, with 20 mills bombs on me … I was down with bullets flying all around me. It was a hard sight. Anyway I kept my head and the first thing that I did was to get clear of the bombs which I rolled from my neck. By that time I was bleeding a lot, most of the blood came out of my mouth on account of me breathing. I knew if I stayed there I would die. So I started to get back … hauling myself along with one arm, for my right arm could not move, and bullets sticking in the ground around me everywhere.

Eventually Osmond managed to reach the British lines and having been bundled off to a casualty clearing station was not one of the sixty-eight who answered their names at roll call next morning.

Look one last time into the park designed by landscape architect Rudolph Cochious, whose son – also Rudolph – was born in Albert in 1923 whilst Rudolph senior worked there, before being educated in Newfoundland and Wakefield in Yorkshire. Rudolph junior was killed in Normandy the day after D-Day whilst serving as a lance corporal with the Cameron Highlanders of Ottowa. How ironic that a man who created one of the most stunning and well-visited 'living' memorials on the Western Front to British Dominion soldiers killed in France should have his own son killed and commemorated in a CWGC cemetery in the same country.

Gaze towards the German line and take a moment to consider the fascinating but ultimately tragic story of Arthur Thomas Charlton of 2/South Wales Borderers, a pre-war collier from Crumlin in South Wales. Wounded in both legs on 24 January 1915, he recovered and embarked for Gallipoli on 10 May in a draft for the 2nd Battalion with which he served until the evacuation.

As detailed in his medical report, on 1 July 1916, Charlton was 'over the parapet, lying down preparatory to advancing and was hit in [the] left foot and right arm by bullets'. He had not moved an inch and the rest of his battalion did not fare much better. As A, C and D companies moved forward they were met by a storm of machine-gun fire and shrapnel. By about 7.30am, according to the war diary, 'the leading companies had lost nearly all officers and about 70% of the men'. The battalion had attacked with 21 officers and 578 men – the diary stating bluntly that 'none reached the enemy's trench'. At roll call that evening losses amounted to 15 officers and 384 men killed, wounded or missing. Arthur Charlton was one of them.

It is hard to imagine, when standing in the green and pleasant surroundings of Newfoundland Park today, but the tragedy that overtook Charlton's battalion occurred in that rough triangle of sloping ground bounded by the path that you have just taken from Y Ravine Cemetery, the German front line and the track leading back to the caribou from the imposing 'Jock' atop the 51st Highland Division Memorial.

Charlton had multiple wounds – 'compound fractures of the right radius, left 2nd, 3rd and 4th metatarsals and 1st phalanges ... tendons and bones exposed on dorsum of foot ... superficial flesh wounds on left side of chest. Necrosis of bones of foot', but after almost a year in hospital he recovered and was discharged in 1919. But his war experiences and the constant pain from his wounds dogged him throughout the 1920s and finally broke him. He gassed himself, aged 47, in March 1931, another victim of 1 July 1916. His widow's pension claim was rejected. For a woman whose husband had served his country in two theatres of war, had been seriously wounded twice and had seen so much violence and endured so much pain, this final indignity must have been a particularly bitter pill to swallow.

Continue along the path towards the entrance. You will pass the visitor's box opposite a poem by William Dunkerley (aka **John Oxenham**) – originally titled 'Vimy Ridge' in his book *High Altars* – the first line of which, 'Tread softly here! Go reverently and slow!' is surely an epitaph for the soldiers of all nations who perished on the Somme in 1916 and the survivors who suffered from its effects in the years that followed. Many who died that day must still lie beneath the soil here.

From the imposing memorial to the 29th Division with its distinctive red triangle, the visitor's centre – opened in 2001– is a short walk away and details the history of the Royal Newfoundland Regiment from 1914. Here there is a memorial room with a copy of the Newfoundland Book of Remembrance and information about a number of personalities who served with the regiment who are portrayed along with other

The 29th Division Memorial.

memorabilia and short video clips. Free guided tours around the memorial park are provided by wonderfully courteous and upbeat Canadian university students trained and sponsored by Veterans Affairs Canada.

At the time of writing access to the Newfoundland Memorial Park is free and the park is open between 28 January and 5 December from 10.00am to 5.00pm, Tuesday to Sunday and 9.00am to 5.00pm on Monday. For information on guided tours email: beaumonthamel. memorial@vac-acc.gc.ca or call +33 (0) 322 767 086. Visitors should note there are no guided tours on Mondays.

Before you leave the park area a brief visit to the car park will reveal a series of seemingly erratic white lines on the tarmac which represent the former position of the **Uxbridge Road** trenches. This is the approximate position where 1/Essex formed up prior to beginning their slow advance through the communication trenches choked with wounded.

After leaving the car park turn left ❻ along the D73 towards Auchonvillers and look just inside the boundary of the Memorial Park to your right. Note the heavily traversed trenches of what was **St John's Road** in 1916. The Newfoundland Regiment formed up and attacked from here before they sky-lined themselves, roughly where the 29th Division Memorial stands today, and came under concentrated machine-gun fire from Y Ravine and the Beaucourt Spur.

On the right, after 250m, you will pass the approximate location of what was marked on many British maps of 1915 as **Thurler's Dump** – later **Thurles** – which served as a medical post on 1 July 1916. Take the next turning on the right ❼ signposted **Hawthorn Ridge Cemetery No. 1**. You are now heading towards Hawthorn Ridge and are behind the British front line of 1 July. The tree-filled crater is almost directly in front of you and the trees of Newfoundland Park are on your right. The track takes you through the former 86 Brigade trenches where 2/Royal Fusiliers and 16/Middlesex were positioned prior to their advance across to the Hawthorn Redoubt. After passing the track on the left, Hawthorn Ridge Cemetery No. 1 comes into view, marked by the two distinctive trees standing either side of the Cross of Sacrifice. In the distance, above Beaumont Hamel, you should be able to make out the two Redan Ridge Cemeteries and Serre Road Cemetery No. 2.

Imagine for a moment the huge explosion of the mine and the lines of British troops emerging from their trenches and crossing the ground on your left. The 2/Royal Fusiliers war diary records that Z Company rushed forward to occupy the crater but fell in droves as the German machine guns opened fire. The general attack along the whole front began 5 minutes later but 'very few of our men reached as far as the enemy barbed wire', an assessment shared by **Captain Guy Goodcliffe**, who was in command of the 10 per cent of the battalion left in reserve. 'The attack was a hopeless failure. As far as I know no-one reached the Bosche front line except a few odd men where the mine was blown. Colonel Johnson – OC the battalion – was buried and wounded by one of our own shells.' On the Fusiliers' left was **Captain Frederick Cockram**, the 16/Middlesex (Public Schools) adjutant, who managed to reach the crater rim before he was hit three times 'collapsing riddled with bullets'. Incredibly, he was one of the few Middlesex officers to survive and spent the remainder of the war as a PoW.

As the track begins to descend the view opens up and the memorial to 8/Argyll and Sutherland Highlanders at the bottom of the **Sunken Road** can be seen. Continue to **Hawthorn Ridge Cemetery No. 1** ❽ on the right. Situated in no-man's-land, the grass pathway leading to this rarely visited cemetery is almost exactly on the British front line of 1 July. Begun by V Corps, which cleared the surrounding battlefields in 1917, there are now 153 casualties commemorated here, over half of which are unidentified. Of the casualties, 42 are men of 16/Middlesex whose costly attack on the Hawthorn Ridge mine crater resulted in 524 officers and men killed, wounded or missing. Amongst their number was 25-year-old **Lieutenant Harold Goodwin** (A.88), the son of the well-known landscape artist Albert Goodwin, and **Second Lieutenant Eric Heaton** (A.89) who gave his name to **Heaton Road Trench** and whose headstone bears the inscription, 'I came out willingly to serve my King and country'. Another Middlesex officer was 21-year-old **Captain George Heslop** (B.40) who enlisted in London and was commissioned in September 1914. He first saw action at Loos in 1915 where he was wounded. Promoted to captain six months later, he was killed on 1 July within 10 minutes of leaving the British front-line trenches. **Corporal Herbert Hosking** (A.85) was born on Christmas Day 1891 and was a student at

Captain George Heslop.

University College School and The Royal College of Music before he enlisted in 16/Middlesex. He was killed on 1 July, as was 20-year-old **Corporal Henry Charles Stephens Rees** (A.68) of Usk, who was with D Company 1/2 Monmouths – the 29th Divisional Pioneers. The men of D Company were split up and attached to several other battalions for the attack and Rees could have been with any one of those that made an abortive attempt to get forward when he went missing.

As you retrace your steps back to the track, take advantage of the views before you turn right towards the Hawthorn mine crater. Continue downhill to where the track appears to stop at a field edge, the crater **9** is on your right and can be accessed by turning right and walking along the field edge. The crater is the result of the mine – then called simply 'H3' – dug by 252/Tunnelling Company under the Hawthorn Redoubt from a shaft sunk in the British support line just over halfway across the field looking due west, between the end of the track here and the line of trees marking the **Old Beaumont Road**. The chamber – at the end of a 300m-long gallery dug a full 25m beneath the ridge – was packed with 40,600lb of ammonal and detonated at 7.20am on 1 July. The mine was dug a little too far north and a little short so when it went up it only took out the trenches at the northwest corner of the redoubt, although the rest of the system suffered severely from the shockwave.

Corporal Henry Charles Stephens Rees.

Apart from alerting the Germans to the imminence of the attack, the huge explosion took half of 1 Platoon, 9 *Kompanie*, RIR 119 – some forty men – up with it. Nearby dugouts collapsed trapping more men who frantically began to dig themselves out and the surviving defenders were – literally – faced with a gaping hole in their defences over 50m in diameter and some 25m deep. For the sure footed it is possible, with great care, to descend into the depths of the crater today where the observant will discern a 'figure of eight' shape left as a result of a second detonation which opened the Battle of the Ancre here on 13 November 1916. On that occasion the old gallery was re-opened and 30,000lb of ammonal was used.

Retrace your steps past Hawthorn Ridge Cemetery and take the track on the right ❿ which you passed earlier. After 450m the track bends round to the right to join the Old Beaumont Road, which descends ahead of you to reach the junction with the D163. Stop here ⓫ and look across the road towards the curved track of **Esau's Way** opposite. This track led up to **White City**, so called because the hundreds of chalky sandbags protecting a large number of dugouts burrowed into the 'safe' lee of the steep bank to the east of the track gleamed white in strong sunlight. The concrete shed you can see is close to the course of a steep section of

The Hawthorn mine crater is marked by a dense thicket of trees and shrubs.

Moments after the detonation of the Hawthorn mine, filmed by Geoffrey Malins on 1 July 1916.

trench called **Jacob's Ladder,** where **Lieutenant Geoffrey Malins**, an official war photographer, filmed the detonation of the Hawthorn Ridge mine, a sequence that became one of the most memorable of the official film *The Battle of the Somme*. Waiting in position at the top of the bank above the concrete shed, he looked at the men around him, laden with equipment and cracking nervous jokes. It was 7.15am:

> Heavens! how the minutes dragged. It seemed like a lifetime waiting there. My nerves were strung up to a high pitch; my heart was thumping like a steam-hammer ... I gave a quick glance at an officer close by. He was mopping the perspiration from his brow ... Would nothing ever happen? ... 7.19 a.m. My hand grasped the handle of the camera. I set my teeth. My whole mind was concentrated upon my work. Another thirty seconds passed. I started turning the handle, two revolutions per second ... I fixed my eyes on the Redoubt. Any second now ... It seemed to me as if I had been turning for hours ... Surely it had not misfired. Why doesn't it go up? I looked at my exposure dial. I had used over a

thousand feet. The horrible thought flashed through my mind, that my film might run out before the mine blew.... The agony was … indescribable … Another 250 feet exposed. I had to keep on. Then it happened. The ground where I stood gave a mighty convulsion. It rocked and swayed. I gripped hold of my tripod to steady myself. Then, for all the world like a gigantic sponge, the earth rose in the air to the height of hundreds of feet. Higher and higher it rose, and with a horrible grinding roar, the earth fell back on itself, leaving in its place a mountain of smoke.

This Jacob's Ladder should not to be confused with the long communication trench of the same name that ran up the hill from Hamel towards Mesnil. Take a minute to walk up the track and climb to the top of Jacob's Ladder and, if you have downloaded the clip of the 'blow' to a tablet or Smartphone, you can get the same view Malins had when he filmed that iconic moment of 'shock and awe'.

After the Germans had retired to the Hindenburg Line the poet 'John Oxenham' stood on the rim of the Hawthorn crater with a friend looking down due east and scanning the blasted wasteland towards the flooded Ancre, to Grandcourt and Miraumont beyond. 'It reminds me of a Scottish moor, ' his companion said, 'but a Scottish moor is full of life and here is nothing but death, death, death.' Perhaps lines from Oxenham's poem 'Beaumont Hamel' should have been the ones chosen for Newfoundland Park rather than the ones we see today:

> 'Is it the sob of the Earth in deadly sorrow
> At the red flood that chokes her hidden ways …?'

Retrace your steps to the main road and turn left, taking the next track after 250m with the CWGC sign for Beaumont Hamel British Cemetery and stop at the imposing **8/Argyll and Sutherland Highlanders Memorial**. ⑫ You are now at the southern end of the famous Sunken Road, another spot immortalized by Malins and roughly halfway across no-man's-land at this point. The 27ft-high Celtic memorial cross stands on the left near where the 8/Argylls battalion HQ was situated during the November 1916 assault on Beaumont Hamel. The inscription on the panel facing you is in Gaelic. 'Cruachan' is the battle cry of the Argylls, taken from a farm of the same name on the west bank of Loch Awe opposite Innis Chonnell Castle – an obvious Clan Campbell rallying point – and the rest translates as 'The Noble Warriors of the Great War – The heroes who went before us'. Tall trees that once surrounded it have now been removed so the area is as it was when it was unveiled by the

Duke of Argyll on 23 March 1923. Note that the memorial was always meant to be viewed first from the other side, with the visitor facing Beaumont Hamel. When the panels are studied from that side the memorial tells its story chronologically, the way it was intended.

Directly opposite is the path leading to **Beaumont Hamel British Cemetery** ⑬ which was originally known as V Corps Cemetery No. 23. The cemetery is halfway again between the Sunken Road and the German front line. Burials began here after the village was captured in November 1916 but on 1 July men of B and D companies, 1/Lancashire Fusiliers, emerged from the Sunken Road to your left and attacked towards you, having 'a few moments grace' before the machine

The 8th Argyll and Sutherland Highlanders Memorial at Beaumont Hamel.

Taken from Hawthorn Ridge, the Sunken Road can be seen sweeping uphill from the Argyll and Sutherland Highlanders' Memorial. The Cross of Sacrifice of Redan Ridge No. 2 Cemetery can be seen on the skyline marked by the line of trees.

guns opened up and they were 'practically wiped out' in the fields all around. There are sixteen of them buried here, including 20-year-old **Private Frank Halliwell** (A.19), one of ten siblings from Chorley in Lancashire where the family worked in the local textile mills. Also, 29-year-old **Private James Knight** (A.61) came from another family of mill workers in Rochdale where his widowed mother Isabella and her six children lived at Broomfield Terrace. Australian-born 22-year-old **Second Lieutenant Arthur Furneaux Anderson** (A.6) is commemorated on the Barrow-in-Furness War Memorial and was commissioned into 4/Lancashire Fusiliers. He landed at Gallipoli in April 1915 with the 1st Battalion surviving long enough to lose his life in the fields surrounding this cemetery on 1 July. Of the seven men of 16/Middlesex buried here 21-year-old **Private Albert Mathama Locke** (A.88) arrived in France in November 1915. The former grocer's boy from London may have been found close to 19-year-old **Private Walter Moody** (A.70) from Mitcham in Surrey and whose name is on the Mitcham War Memorial. A former banking clerk with Southern Railways, his widowed mother and eldest sister both worked in the local laundry.

Return to the Sunken Road – also occasionally known as **Hunter Trench** – which achieved notoriety in Malins' film when he captured the wide-eyed faces of the Lancashire Fusiliers sheltering in it a few hours prior to their attack on 1 July. During the day the road was too vulnerable to hostile fire but the Fusiliers had access to it via a shallow tunnel – Sap 7 – and communication trench dug by 1/2 Monmouths from the British front line on the ridge behind the memorial which was completed by 2.30am on 1 July. The opening of this tunnel in the western bank towards the top end of the lane is hard to discern today, although the observant amongst you will pick out the last vestiges of numerous excavations into the banks.

Lieutenant Colonel Meredith Magniac had ordered B and D companies to steal a march on the Germans by moving through the tunnel and occupying the Sunken Road as an advanced jumping off line from which they would rush the German line under the cover of the artillery barrage, leaving his remaining men to follow on behind. Malins took his camera through Sap 7 and filmed them here. Look up and down this now peaceful lane and imagine the scene as Malins saw it:

The tunnel was no more than two feet six inches wide and five feet high … The journey seemed endless … I dragged my camera along by the strap attached to the case … At last we came to the exit … 'Keep down low, sir. This sap is only four feet deep.' My guide was crouching there, and in front of him, about thirty feet away, running at right angles on both sides, was a roadway, overgrown with grass and pitted with shell-holes. The bank immediately in front was lined with the stumps of trees and a rough hedge, and there lined up, crouching as close to the bank as possible, were some of our men. They were the Lancashire Fusiliers, with bayonets fixed, and ready to spring forward … I set my camera up and … filmed the waiting Fusiliers. Some of them looked happy and gay, others sat with stern, set faces, realising the great task in front of them. I … finished taking my scenes … Packing up my camera, I prepared to return. Time was getting on. It was now 6.30am.

Sadly, the Fusiliers were victims of the early detonation of the Hawthorn mine and another obstacle – a *remblai*, or lynchet, which you can see towards the trees from the northeast corner of the cemetery – and were cut down within a few metres of scrambling out of the Sunken Road. **Corporal George Ashurst** was with the second wave:

It's time to go over the top. It was partly blown down and I'm just stepping on top, there was a corporal lying there, gone all blown away, I think he'd been hit by a whizz-bang. He looks up at me as I passed him, 'Go on Corporal, get the bastards!' There were bullets everywhere. Run, that was the only thing in my mind. Run and dodge. Expecting at any second to get hit, to feel a bullet hit me. I was zig-zagging, holding my head down so a bullet would hit my tin hat, I seemed to be dodging in between them, I must have been to get there! There was gun smoke. You could hear when a bullet hit somebody, you could hear it hit him! Hear him groan and go down. It was mainly machine guns that cut us up. I was thinking, I've got to get forward that's all. I dived into the Sunken Road. Picking myself up and looking around, my God, what a sight! The whole of the road was strewn with dead and dying men.

Within 45 minutes the lane was a scene of utter confusion. As you continue walking uphill, imagine the chaos of battle unfolding around you as Lieutenant Colonel Magniac attempts to reorganize survivors to attack the northern end of Beaumont Hamel. Ashurst heard the colonel 'calling out for all fit men to line the bank of the road, waving his revolver menacingly as he did so'. The war diary records that some men 'encumbered by coils of wire, mauls etc' had been hit on the bank and 'rolled down this to the bottom' to join the dead and about 100 wounded in addition to others who had moved up from the British front line to push on. Another attack was launched from the top end of the lane at 8.45am which was also repulsed amidst a hail of shrapnel and enemy gun fire. Ashurst recalled that 'hundreds of dead lay about, and wounded men were trying to crawl back to safety, their heart rending cries could be heard above the noise of rifle fire and bursting shells'.

Continue uphill and at the junction of tracks turn right onto what was known as **Watling Street** towards Beaumont Hamel. After 80m the long grass pathway leading to **Redan Ridge No. 2 Cemetery** appears on your left. The cemetery ⑭ was begun by V Corps in 1917 when the surrounding battlefields were cleared and is situated about 90m west of the 1 July German front line. Today there are over 250 graves

Second Lieutenant Reginald Anderson.

of which approximately 100 are unidentified. Four second lieutenants who were all killed on 1 July are buried in the first row in front of the Cross of Sacrifice. Commissioned in June 1915, **Henry Alexander** (C.8) was amongst the 100 per cent officer casualties sustained by 1/Hampshires. Buried nearby is 20-year-old **Reginald Anderson** (C.4) who initially served as a sergeant before being commissioned into the York and Lancaster Regiment. CWGC information on this man is incorrect as he was killed near John Copse opposite Serre whilst serving with A Company, 14/York and Lancs (2nd Barnsley Pals) on 1 July which means he is buried some distance from where he was posted as missing. His elder brother, Lieutenant Bernard Anderson, was awarded the MC and died of wounds in August 1916 serving with 10/Lincolnshires, and a third brother, Arthur, served with the RFA and survived the war. Commissioned in March 1915, 21-year-old **Frank Anderton** (C.33) was killed in 1/Lancashire Fusiliers' attack from the Sunken Road. **Henry Grant** (C.31) may well have been one of the three subalterns from A Company, 1/Lancashire Fusiliers, who were hit in the advance to the Sunken Road; his company commander, 23-year-old **Captain Edward Matthey** (C.44) was killed a few minutes later. Matthey was admitted to Sandhurst in September 1912 from Cheltenham College and commissioned in January 1913. Finally, visit the grave of 36-year-old **Corporal George Mills** MM (A.17) who was killed with 1/Hampshires on 1 July: the inscription on his headstone reads, 'For God, King and Country'.

From the cemetery turn left towards the junction with the Rue de la Montagne **15** which is part of the Spine Route from Serre to Beaumont Hamel. Continue downhill to the junction with the D163 where you will find the 51st Highland Division flagpole on the right on the way to your vehicle at the church.

Beaumont Hamel to the Ulster Tower

Distance: 6.6km/4.1 miles
Suitable for: 🚗 🚲

From the church at Beaumont Hamel return to the crossroads with the D163 and turn left towards Auchonvillers, passing the 51st Division Flagpole and the 8/Argyll and Sutherland Highlanders Memorial, to arrive at the Auchonvillers crossroads. Turn left onto the D73 signposted **Menisl-Martinsart** and **Newfoundland Park Battlefield Memorial**, the village war memorial is on the left and **Avril Williams' Ocean Villa Guest House & Tea Rooms** further along the road on the right. Drive through the village bearing left at the junction to find **Auchonvillers Communal Cemetery** on the left where there is parking opposite.

On the far left perimeter of the cemetery, almost hidden by a beech hedge, are a row of fifteen casualties, thirteen of them of 1/Border Regiment who were killed on 6 April 1916 when a sudden German bombardment fell on their trenches. The headstones are unusually constructed from red Corsehill or Locharbriggs sandstone, further examples of which can also be found in **Martinsart British Cemetery** to the north of Albert. On 1 July a further 619 officers and men of 1/Border Regiment became casualties near **Y Ravine**. Also in the cemetery is the grave of **William Brown** (1896–1954), who was the first caretaker of the Newfoundland Memorial Park.

Leave the cemetery continuing along the D73 past Newfoundland Memorial Park to catch sight of the **Thiepval Memorial to the Missing** almost immediately ahead on top

Private Thomas Goodman was one of thirteen men from the 1st Border Regiment killed on 6 April 1916.

of the ridge across the Ancre valley. As the road descends and passes under the line of electricity pylons look across to your left to where the British front line meandered its way across the landscape. It was about 450m to your left that the British salient named the **Mary Redan** was situated. A better view can be obtained further down the road where there is some verge-side parking. As the road bends round to the right you should be able to see Mill Road snaking up towards the Ulster Tower on the opposite side of the valley. At the T-Junction turn left onto the D50. Should you wish to visit

Lieutenant Geoffrey Cather VC.

Ancre British Cemetery you will find it 350m further along the road on the left just beyond the point where the British line bulged towards the Germans in what was known as the **William Redan**, complementing the Mary Redan further north. The cemetery lies in the shallow Vallée Saillant which was where **Lieutenant Geoffrey Cather** of 9/Royal Irish Fusiliers was killed on 2 July 1916 bringing three men back to the safety of British lines. The next morning he brought in another wounded man but was killed shortly afterwards. His posthumous award of the **Victoria Cross** was gazetted in September 1916.

Burials began here after the German withdrawal to the Hindenburg Line in February 1917 at which point the cemetery contained 517 burials, mainly of men from the 36th Ulster and 63rd Royal Naval divisions before it was greatly expanded with casualties from the surrounding battlefields. The majority of those buried in the cemetery died on 1 July, 3 September or 13 November 1916. There are now 2,540 casualties buried or commemorated in the cemetery of which over half are unidentified. Special memorials commemorate forty-three casualties known or believed to be buried amongst them and there are a further sixteen special memorials to men known to have been buried in other cemeteries. Amongst these is **Private James Atwill** (Sp Mem 37) of 1/Newfoundland Regiment, who was killed on 1 July. His body was one of those brought in after the battlefield clearances, possibly from the former Y Ravine Cemetery No. 2. Another Newfoundlander is 27-year-old **Captain Eric Ayre** (II.E.12) from St John's, whose brother, Bernard – buried in Carnoy Military Cemetery – was also killed on 1 July serving with 8/Norfolks. Three other members of the Ayre family were killed on that tragic day, 19-year-old Lance Corporal Edward Ayre (Y Ravine Cemetery), 25-year-old Second Lieutenant Gerald Ayre

(Newfoundland Memorial) and 21-year-old Second Lieutenant Wilfred Ayre (**Knightsbridge Cemetery**).

One of the most well known of the November casualties was 21-year-old **Lieutenant Hon. Vere Harmsworth** (V.E.19) of the Hawke Battalion RND. He was the son of Lord Rothermere and was killed at the Beaucourt Redoubt on 13 November 1916. The RND – formed from mainly naval reservists with the addition of Kitchener volunteers – captured Beaucourt and the Beaucourt Spur during the last days of the Battle of the Ancre in November 1916 and their memorial, which was unveiled in 1922, can be seen in Beaucourt-sur-Ancre. When the RND Memorial Committee was seeking financial assistance to place a monument at Beaucourt Lord Rothermere offered to provide the necessary funding. Vere Harmsworth's brother, Harold, died of wounds whilst serving with 2/Irish Guards in February 1918. He is buried in Hampstead Cemetery, London (WB.620).

After leaving the cemetery retrace your route to the junction and turn left to cross the railway line following the CWGC sign for **36th (Ulster) Division Memorial**. You are now on Mill Road and about to cross the River Ancre. It is worth remembering that not long after the British arrived on the Somme in the summer of 1915, the entire frontage from north of John Copse at Serre all the way down to this point – the responsibility of three divisions on 1 July 1916 – was held by just two brigades of the 4th Division!

If you want to park your vehicle there is space near the two bridges that span the various pools of the Ancre. Walk up to the second bridge and look upstream to the weir where the former mill was situated. The low-lying ground in the valley floor prevented the digging of trenches. The Germans had tackled the problem by felling the abundant timber to construct what amounted to a lengthy wooden barricade, which they aptly named the *Biber Kolonie* **(Beaver Colony)**, some 500m upstream from the mill. The British relied upon a series of posts garrisoned by small parties of men to defend the line. Three of these outposts were positioned near the ruined mill whilst others such as **Lancashire Post, Burnt House and Signal Box** protected the south face of William Redan this side of the railway. **Caester Post** was 300m downstream of this bridge. Lieutenant Commander Frederick Kelly, who, like Vere Harmsworth was killed on 13 November 1916, was right here in October 1916: '[My] B Company is on the right and holds posts with sentry groups dotted about in the marshy ground on the Ancre, half-way between Hamel and St-Pierre-Divion. Their names are "Bastion", "Picturedrome"– both on slightly higher ground a few yards to the west of the railway – "Lancashire", "Crow's Nest" and "Corner Post" to the

The site of the former mill on the Ancre is almost obscured by the invading vegetation.

east of the railway; and "Bridge Post" and "Mill Post" – the former only held at night – just by the Ancre.' Originally buried in Hamel, Kelly now lies in **Martinsart British Cemetery** (1.H.25).

Continue up what was called **Mill Road** towards the Ulster Tower, which comes into view up ahead. Mill Road was in no-man's-land on 1 July with the German front-line trenches 150m off to your left and the British front line skirting the eastern edge of Thiepval Wood to your right. Park outside the Ulster Tower.

Route 6

The Thiepval Spur

A circular tour beginning at: **Ulster Tower**
Coordinates: **50°03'38.57" N – 2°40'46.75" E**
Distance: **7.9km/4.9 miles**
Suitable for: ♦ ⚲
Grade: **Moderate (total ascent 113m)**
Toilets: **Ulster Tower and Thiepval Visitor Centre**
Maps: **IGN Série Bleue 2407O – Acheux-en-Amiénois**

General description and context: This route looks at the X Corps
1 July attacks made by the 36th (Ulster) Division on the Ancre heights
and the 32nd Division's assault on Thiepval. The roots of the formation
of the 36th Division lay in the fears of Unionists sparked by the
proposed Irish Home Rule Bill, which was eventually introduced in
April 1912. These fears led to the formation of local volunteer 'militias'
which, in 1913, were organized into the paramilitary Ulster Volunteer
Force (UVF). The outbreak of war in 1914 saw the UVF units forming
the 36th Division and arriving in France during October 1915. On
1 July the division was commanded by **Major General Oliver Nugent**,
whose battle headquarters was at **Gordon Castle** in Thiepval Wood
(Bois d'Authuille). The 32nd Division, commanded by **Major General
William Rycroft**, was a 'New Army' Division composed largely of
Pals battalions but with a 'stiffening' of 'regulars' such as 1/Dorsets and
2/KOYLI – with which one of the author's great-uncles was serving.

The X Corps front line ran from the boundary with III Corps in Authuille
Wood (Bois de la Haie), north along the lower slopes of Thiepval Ridge to
continue in front of Thiepval Wood before crossing the Ancre River to the
boundary with VIII Corps at Mary Redan. On 1 July X Corps was tasked
with the capture of the entire Thiepval Ridge and plateau, which would
enable the British to overlook the German front north towards Serre
and south to Contalmaison. Success depended upon the 32nd Division
taking Thiepval village and the **Leipzig Salient** with the 36th Division
capturing the plateau between Thiepval village and the village of
St-Pierre-Divion, 500m northeast of Mill Road. This task included seizing
– and holding – the **Schwaben Redoubt** – a trench system known as

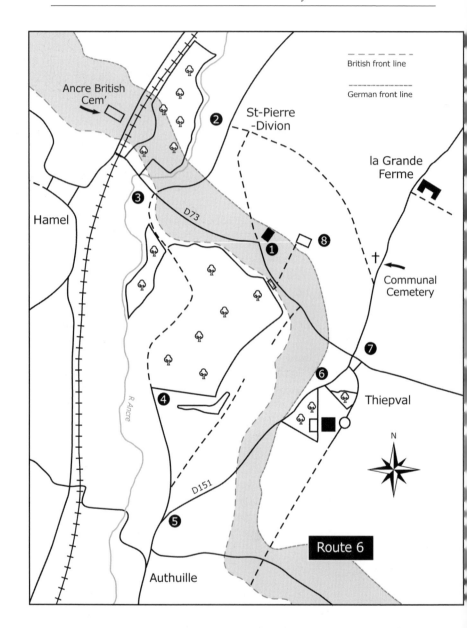

British front line

German front line

Ancre British Cem'

St-Pierre -Divion

la Grande Ferme

Hamel

D73

Communal Cemetery

Thiepval

R Ancre

N

D151

Route 6

Authuille

Feste Schwaben by the Germans and which took up the southernmost third of a trench system the British referred to as **The Quadrilateral** or, as it appeared on Major General Nugent's map at least, as **The Parallelogram**. This system was the 'vital ground' of the entire sector of the German 26th Reserve Division, dominating the ground to the northwest on either side of the Ancre valley, towards Beaucourt up to Beaumont Hamel and even the Redan Ridge beyond. The Germans would not give it up lightly!

After these initial successes the two divisions were to cross the plateau and take the German third-line trenches – the **Mouquet Switch** and the **Hansa Line** – and consolidate whilst the 49th Division units moved through to attack the Mouquet Farm–Grandcourt line.

Major General Oliver Nugent.

The 36th Division's assault was very successful, except on the left flank where, north of the Ancre, 12/Royal Irish Rifles and 9/Royal Irish Fusiliers of 108 Brigade moved forward with the 29th Division towards Beaucourt and failed to advance beyond the German front line. South of the river 13/ Royal Irish Rifles was almost wiped out by machine-gun fire directed from the Beaucourt Spur and St-Pierre-Divion but 11/ Royal Irish Rifles managed to make better progress and by 8.15am many of them had reached the southern face of the Schwaben Redoubt. On their right the 9 and 10/Royal Inniskilling Fusiliers from 109 Brigade overpowered the German front-line defenders before they could open fire. Despite coming under heavy machine-gun fire from the south from Thiepval, men from both battalions were fighting in the Schwaben Redoubt by around 8.00am. By 10.30am scattered groups from 107 Brigade were within 75m of their third objective, the Mouquet Farm–Grandcourt line, and even though 200 men reached **Battery Valley**, 500m or so beyond, the greater part of 107 Brigade and the surviving men of 108 and 109 brigades were now pinned down by German machine-gun fire.

The Germans brought up reinforcements and fierce, well-organized counter-attacks started to develop by the early afternoon and continued into the night. These, together with artillery and machine-gun fire preventing any reinforcements from crossing no-man's-land, forced the surviving Ulstermen to withdraw. Their casualties exceeded 5,400 officers and men, outstripping the 4,000 casualties suffered by the 32nd Division in its unsuccessful attack on Thiepval.

Directions to start: The Ulster Tower is situated on the D73 between Hamel and Thiepval. Park outside the tower but be aware that the available space is sometimes used by large coaches and other tourist vehicles.

Route description: Before you begin the tour walk through to the rear of the Ulster Tower grounds and look across the bare expanse of the Thiepval Ridge. This is the ground over which the 36th Division attacked on 1 July 1916 and had it been possible to establish a relatively secure line from Mill Road across to the Schwaben Redoubt along which fresh supplies of ammunition and reinforcements could have been ferried forward, the Thiepval stronghold may well have been compromised. As it was, the message received by **Lieutenant Colonel William Savage**, commanding 13/Royal Irish Fusiliers, from **Captain James Davidson** – whose grave we visited in Serre Road Cemetery No. 2 – summed up the failure of a courageous assault by the Ulstermen against a strong and tenacious enemy: 'Am in B line and have got up two Vickers guns, am consolidating both. Cannot say how many infantry are in line, but in this part there are only about 30 men of the 13th, 11th, and 15th Royal Irish Rifles. We cannot possibly advance and reinforcements, ammunition and bombs most urgently needed.'

The Ulster Tower is a stunning replica of a tower that was dedicated by Lord Dufferin to his mother Helen in 1867 and which still stands today on the Dufferin and Ava Estate at Clandeboye in County Down, where the 36th Ulster Division trained prior to its departure for England in 1915. Designed by Bowden and Abbot of Craven Street, London, it was built in 1921 by Fenning and Company Ltd of Hammersmith, London and the Société de Construction et Travaux Publics d'Arras. The tower stands approximately 21m high and is under the management of the Somme Association – based in Craigavon House, Belfast – and boasts a visitor centre housing a small museum and where refreshments, books and souvenirs can be purchased. The tower is open to the public from Tuesday to Sunday, 10.00am to 6.00pm, May–September and from 10.00am to 5.00pm, March, April, October and November. Admission is free as is access to the memorial chapel in the base of the tower. At the time of writing (autumn 2015) visits to the former Ulster Division trenches in Thiepval Wood can be arranged through the staff at the tower. There is no fee but a donation that recognizes the unique access to the site and the deep knowledge of the guide will be greatly appreciated.

With the entrance gates to the Ulster Tower on your right ❶ take the farm track that heads downhill into the Ancre valley towards St-Pierre-

Divion. Take care not to block this route with your vehicle as it is used regularly by farm machinery. After 100m the remains of a **German observation post** can be seen on the right, marked by several lengths of railway track. Situated on the German front line, which ran left to right across the track in front of you, this post overlooked the British line and marked the position of a German salient called the **Pope's Nose**. It is worth noting that the track you are now standing on was how Mill Road would have looked in July 1916.

Continue downhill, crossing the former positions of the German second and third lines of defence to turn left at the junction. Pass the private house on the left to the church, around which was constructed a strongpoint known as the *Pfalzburger*

The Ulster Tower.

Part of the reconstructed 36th Division trenches in Thiepval Wood.

The track leading downhill to St-Pierre-Divion from the Ulster Tower with the Beaucourt spur beyond the ridge in the middle distance.

Stellung. Continue to the junction ❷ turning left into the village of St-Pierre-Divion, which was defended by IR 66. The narrow tree-lined Route de St-Pierre-Divion now runs parallel with the Ancre River towards Mill Road.

After 200m stop and look across the river. At this point you are opposite **Ancre British Cemetery**. **Summer House Post** was some 150m in front of you and the **Picturedrome** and **Lancashire Posts** were on the far side of the river near the railway line. The German trench line would have been above the bank on your left. German maps suggest there were four entrances here which led to an underground network of tunnels and dugouts connected to the trenches above by stairways. The largest is said to have been capable of housing up to 1,000 men. Jack Sheldon is of the opinion that there is no documentary evidence to suggest that this underground system was ever connected to the Schwaben Redoubt by a network of tunnels or that any such tunnels existed below the redoubt itself. As the road nears the junction with Mill Road you will see a private house on the left, beyond which was no-man's-land; a foray up into the overgrown area on the left will reveal the remnants of the German front-line trenches and the remains of the old

The road leading from St-Pierre-Divion towards Thiepval Wood is bordered on the right by the River Ancre.

quarry. As you continue towards Mill Road the views open out towards **Thiepval Wood** which you can see directly ahead. St-Pierre-Divion was eventually captured by units of the 39th Division on 13 November 1916.

At the junction with Mill Road ❸ stop. Imagine for a moment that it is just after 7.15am on 1 July 1916 and you are standing in the middle of no-man's-land. A glance to your left reveals long lines of Ulstermen lying in the road waiting for the signal to begin their assault, well aware that the day marked the original anniversary – before the Gregorian superseded the Julian calendar – of the Battle of the Boyne fought 226 years earlier. There is an enduring mythology that many men wore orange sashes to mark the event but no firm documentary evidence has come to light in the records of the units involved. A few contemporary accounts record that some men saw others wearing the odd orange sash, carrying an orange handkerchief – one such reported as being **Major George Gaffikin** of 9/Royal Irish Rifles – or even wearing orange lilies and it is entirely likely that a few men may have carried such tokens for personal encouragement or for 'good luck' but it seems certain it was not a widespread phenomenon.

The 13/Royal Irish Rifles moved into Mill Road at 7.15am and began their advance uphill several minutes before zero in order to be within 50m of the German front line when the British artillery barrage lifted. **Lieutenant Colonel William Savage**, observing his battalion's progress from **Peterhead Sap**, noted that, 'directly the start was made the German machine guns could be heard firing at once'. The battalion was met with a wave of machine-gun fire which cut them down 'like sheaves of corn on the ground'. Serving with C Company was **Captain Charles Murland**, a great-uncle of one of the authors, who was hit even before he reached the German first line. In a letter written from Forceville on 8 July he described how he watched his boyhood friends being scythed down around him, one of those was **Major Albert Uprichard**, who commanded D Company. 'I saw Albert go down at the head of his company but was unable to reach him before he died.' A glance behind you will give you almost the same view as men of 108 Brigade had on the morning of 1 July with the German front line running from the tip of the trees bordering the open fields up to the row of trees bordering the Ulster Tower. Later in the morning the same

Old Comrades of 13/Royal Ulster Rifles gathered together at Ballygowan in 1960. Captain Charles Murland is standing at the front on the right.

road would be strewn with corpses and wounded men, earning it the nickname the 'Bloody Road'.

Directly opposite a track – known as **Speyside Road** – bears round to the left and into Thiepval Wood. Take this track and stop where it begins to rise and where there is a small clearing on the right. Beyond the clearing is where the British front line ran parallel to Mill Road with **Burghead Sap** on the bank above and **Peterhead Sap** further to the right. These positions were the last of the formal trenches before the marshes of the Ancre valley. Continue along the track, which can be very muddy in wet weather, noting the steep bank on the left which undoubtedly contained entrances to British dugouts. These steep slopes were very probably the site of many of the Ulster Division's field kitchens and where the 15/Royal Irish Rifles would have been assembled waiting to support the 108 Brigade attack. The first of four Victoria Crosses awarded to individuals in the 36th Division was won in this area half an hour before zero on 1 July. In an act of supreme self-scarifice **Private Billy McFadzean,** serving with the 14/Royal Irish Rifles, threw himself on two grenades that had accidentally been dropped, killing himself in the process but saving the lives of those who were with him.

As the track begins to bend round to the left, look right across the Ancre valley. The railway line will probably be obscured by foliage but it was approximately here that one of several causeways built across the Ancre valley – the **Passerelle de Magenta** – provided a route from Mesnil to the British front line. Two causeways to either side were built with sandbags filled with chalk by 16/Royal Irish Rifles. A little further on the 1/5 and 1/6 West Yorks from 146 Brigade crossed the Ancre via the South Causeway just after 10.00am on 1 July after leaving **Aveluy Wood** prior to their 4.00pm attack on Thiepval. The light railway built to transport stores and ammunition up to the 36th Division ran along the western edge of the wood from Authuille and later served to facilitate the removal of the wounded to the advanced dressing station in Aveluy Wood. No trace of this remains today.

Eventually, a small private house next to the Etang Glavieux comes into view on the right and after 250m the track breaks out into the fields ahead ❹ then curves away to the right. Stop here. The Thiepval Memorial to the Missing is visible to the left on the ridge beyond the shallow valley with the long expanse of **Caterpillar Wood** on the right. Directly ahead the line of poplars on the skyline marks the position of the *Granatloch* – a disused quarry or claypit some 60m long and 40 wide – which stands at the tip of the German-held **Leipzig Salient**.

Looking up the valley towards the Thiepval Memorial from the southwestern corner of Thiepval Wood. Caterpillar Wood in on the right.

Continue along the track for 350m to cross over into the sector held by the 32nd Division. To the left of the track is the forming up point of 2/Royal Inniskilling Fusiliers just south of Caterpillar Wood; the four companies moving off between 8.55am and 11.00am. This is a good spot from which to view the ground over which 96 Brigade attacked on 1 July. The 15/Lancashire Fusiliers (1st Salford Pals) attacked Thiepval directly uphill from the eastern edge of Thiepval Wood into uncut wire and heavy machine-gun fire, and II/RIR 99 had little trouble repelling their attack. On their right flank the 16/Northumberland Fusiliers (Tyneside Commercials) were largely shot down before they even reached the German first line, the war diary recording that many of their men were found later lying in 'straight lines of ten or twelve dead or badly wounded as if the platoon had been dressed for parade'.

The track – which is now metalled – continues to run alongside the Ancre valley and almost parallel with the British front line, rising gently towards the village of Authuille. As you near the top of the hill, ignore the track leading off to the left. This track, which passes the former **Johnstone Post** on the southeastern angle of Thiepval Wood, has been ploughed up at its far end and no longer connects with the D73 west of Thiepval. However, a short detour up the track to see around the bend will enable you to look towards that point marked approximately by the mass of trees in the distance. It was from Johnstone Post at 9.15am that two companies of 16/Lancashire Fusiliers (2nd Salford Pals) were ordered by **Brigadier General Clement Yatman**, commanding 96 Brigade, to advance in support of 15/Lancashire Fusiliers, who were thought to be in Thiepval village, and by so doing bridge the gap to the Ulstermen fighting in the Schwaben Redoubt. Not a single man made it across no-man's-land and those who were not killed were compelled to withdraw.

Continue for another 170m to the junction with the D151. You are now standing directly above the site of **Yatman Bridge** which crossed the Ancre down the slope to your right. On 1 July the units of 107 Brigade left Aveluy Wood and crossed the bridge on their way to Speyside Road before moving through the forest rides towards the front line. Authuille – which we visit during the **Ulster Tower to Ovillers-la-Boisselle Spine Route** – is 300m down the hill ahead of you.

Turn left ❺ and continue uphill towards Thiepval and its memorial, which can be seen on the skyline. The road rises gradually and after 700m you will see two short tracks giving access to the fields on the right marking the approximate position of the British front line that ran left to right across the road. The German front line was 300m further on. Across the fields on your left – east of Caterpillar Wood – is where the Lancashire and Northumberland Fusiliers (NF) formed up before their advance.

On the brow of the hill, almost opposite the Thiepval Memorial, is the memorial to the 18th Division ❻ which finally took the village at the end of September 1916. This is a superb spot from which to view the surrounding area, it being at 140m above sea level and the highest point of the route. Stand with the Thiepval Memorial behind you. Down the slope ahead you can see the **Connaught Cemetery** on the eastern edge of Thiepval Wood and to its right the Ulster Tower and Mill Road. To the right of the Ulster Tower on the skyline are the trees surrounding **Mill Road Cemetery**, which is situated on the German front line and west of the **Schwaben Redoubt**. In the immediate foreground to your right are the farm buildings which now stand on the approximate site of the **Chateau Grand Sapin – Thiepval Chateau**, which, apart from its cellarage, had been totally destroyed by July 1916. This was also the site of the final German stand on 26 September 1916 from where the defenders were finally pushed back towards the Schwaben Redoubt. It was up the slope from the wood directly in front of you that 15/ and two companies of 16/Lancashire Fusiliers attacked on 1 July and the ground below you would have been covered with the dead and dying of those battalions.

We suggest you leave a visit to the Thiepval Memorial and its visitor centre until later as we will be passing this way again on our way to Ovillers-la-Boisselle.

Continue straight on to the church where a memorial plaque to **Lieutenant General Sir Adrian Carton de Wiart VC** (see **Route 8**) can be seen to the right of the entrance. Thiepval was captured without a shot being fired by II/IR 121 in September 1914 and the church was initially used by the men of IR 180 in the first months of the war, a practice that was discontinued in early November 1914 as the building came under regular shell fire.

The 18th Division Memorial.

From the church continue to the cross roads and turn left ❼ on the D73 towards St-Pierre-Divion following the CWGC signpost

The plaque commemorating Sir Adrian Carton de Wiart at Thiepval church.

for Connaught and Mill Road Cemeteries. As the road descends **Connaught Cemetery** comes into view on the left. Park outside the entrance. Immediately behind the cemetery is Thiepval Wood and it was across the ground now occupied by the cemetery that 10/Royal Inniskilling Fusiliers of 109 Brigade advanced towards the German front line which was where Mill Road Cemetery stands today. Later in the afternoon C and D companies of 1/7 West Yorks – The Leeds Rifles – also traversed this ground.

Connaught Cemetery was begun during the early autumn of 1916 and at the Armistice it contained 228 burials. Like so many cemeteries in the area, it was expanded when graves were brought in from the surrounding battlefields and smaller cemeteries. There are now 1,268 burials here of which half are unidentified. Special memorials commemorate two casualties believed to be buried here and five from the former Divion Wood Cemetery No. 2. **Captain Ernest McLaren** (I.B.22) served with 15/Lancashire Fusiliers (1st Salford Pals) and was captain of the Western Cricket Club in Pendleton. A noted horseman, he was awarded the Military Cross for successfully carrying out a raid on enemy trenches the previous year. He was killed on 1 July with 30-year-old Pendleton-born **Sergeant William Mountain** (I.B.12) who served in the same battalion. **Captain Charles Slacke** (IV.A.9) of 14/Royal Irish Fusiliers was killed – aged 44 – leading his men towards the Schwaben

Connaught Cemetery.

Redoubt. The son of Sir Owen Randal Slacke, he was married to Kate who placed the Slacke Memorial commemorating her husband's death in St John's Church, Newcastle, County Down. Serving in the same battalion was 19-year-old **Rifleman Arthur Morrow** (III.M.4) from Belfast who was the only son of John and Mary Morrow. It is not known whether he was one of those Belfast 'Young Citizens' which overpowered the German defenders in the Schwaben Redoubt but he was originally posted as missing before his death on 1 July was confirmed several weeks later.

Sergeant William Mountain.

Opposite the cemetery entrance a long track takes you to **Mill Road Cemetery ❽** which was originally called Mill Road Cemetery No. 2 and was begun when the battlefield was cleared after the German withdrawal to the Hindenburg Line. From the back of the cemetery there are excellent views of the ground over which the 36th Division attacked on 1 July. At the Armistice it contained 260 burials but was then enlarged with graves brought in from the battlefields of Beaumont Hamel and Thiepval and smaller surrounding cemeteries. There are now 1,304 casualties buried here of which 815 are unidentified. The majority of the original burials have their headstones laid flat due to the unstable nature of the ground whilst those that were brought in later were buried in firmer ground and have upright headstones. The graves are predominately from those units that fought in and around Thiepval.

One of the two senior officers buried here is 36-year-old **Major Albert Uprichard** (X.C.8) who commanded D Company of 13/Royal Irish Rifles and was the managing director of the Belfast Company, Forster and Green Co. One of three brothers, the family owned and ran the Springvale Bleach Works in the Bann Valley, County Down. Banbridge-born 24-year-old **Lieutenant George Rogers** (II.D.5) of the 13/Royal Irish Rifles was another Ulsterman whose family was involved in the linen industry. On the outbreak of war he was managing family business interests in Courtrai but successfully avoided the advancing German Army to return home where he was commissioned in November 1914. Another Ulsterman was 31-year-old **Captain James Proctor** (IX.D.9) who was educated at Reading School in Berkshire and Trinity College, Dublin before he trained as a solicitor. On the outbreak of war he was gazetted captain in 10/Royal Inniskilling Fusiliers in

Mill Road Cemetery.

September 1914 and died of wounds on 1 July. Serving with A Company Heavy Branch Machine Gun Corps, 22-year-old **Lieutenant Herbert Hitchcock** (II.B.10) commanded A13, one of the first tanks to go into battle on the Western Front. He was killed on 13 November during the successful attack on St-Pierre-Divion by the 39th Division. Buried next to him is one of his crew members, Birmingham-born **Gunner William Miles** (II.B.9) who later became a window cleaner in Coventry where he married Mary Troop in 1914. He was a member of the former Barras Working Men's Club in the centre of Coventry and was killed with Hitchcock on 13 November. Before you leave, spend a moment at the grave of 32-year-old **Rifleman Robert Watson** of the 13/Royal Irish Fusiliers. Born in Lurgan, he lived in Victoria Street with his parents and younger sister Sara. Described on the 1911 Census return as a 'van man',

Major Albert Uprichard.

he was still single when he volunteered for service on the outbreak of war. His death on 1 July was one of the 595 casualties sustained by his battalion on 1 July. Leave the cemetery and continue to the Ulster Tower for some well-earned refreshment.

Front Line Spine Route
Ulster Tower to Ovillers-la-Boisselle

Distance: 5.5km/3.4 miles
Suitable for: 🚗 🚲

During this short route we provide an opportunity to visit three CWGC Cemeteries, the site of the Schwaben Redoubt, the Thiepval Memorial to the Missing and look more closely at the 32nd Division assault on the Leipzig Salient.

From the Ulster Tower head back up Mill Road towards Thiepval and at the crossroads near the church turn left to visit the site of the **Schwaben Redoubt**, the eastern tip of which is marked by the buildings of **la Grande Ferme,** which, at 153m above sea level, represents the highest point on the Thiepval Ridge. For a better view park your vehicle by the triangular shaped communal cemetery situated in the small copse on the left of the road (see **Route 6** Map) and walk up the track to its left following the line of a German communication trench called *Strassburgher Steige* (slope) to St-Pierre-Divion. Your arrival at the site of the Schwaben Redoubt will be confirmed by the superb views that open

The communal cemetery on the D151.

up to the west, dominating the ground that the 36th Division advanced through on 1 July as it slides down into the Ancre valley and beyond. It was in the vicinity of the redoubt that two Victoria Crosses were won on 1 July. The first was awarded to **Captain Eric Bell**, commanding the 109 Brigade Trench Mortar Battery, for rallying parties of soldiers whose officers had become casualties. Prior to this he had silenced a German machine-gun post. He was killed soon afterwards. The second was awarded to **Corporal George Sanders** of 1/7 West Yorks who advanced with C and D companies at 3.30pm with orders to support 107 Brigade in holding the Schwaben Redoubt. Although the Ulstermen were driven back by about 10.30pm, Saunders rescued some prisoners who had been captured in the earlier fighting and, finding himself isolated,

Corporal George Sanders VC after promotion to sergeant.

organized his party of thirty or so men and drove off repeated German attacks. Fortunately, he was relieved on 2 July and brought nineteen men back to British lines.

Retrace your route and on your return to the communal cemetery glance across to the left, a long communication trench – *Martinspfad* – ran east of the D151 from the southeastern tip of the redoubt down to Thiepval. Return to the crossroads in Thiepval and follow the CWGC signposts to the **Thiepval Memorial Visitor Centre** which was opened in September 2004 on the eighty-eighth anniversary of the day that the 18th Division finally forced the remnants of the 26th (Würtemburg) Division out of the eastern edge of the village. The visitor centre welcomes over 150,000 visitors each year and provides an overview of the course of the First World War from 1914–18. At the time of writing work was ongoing to build a museum extension at ground level in time for the centenary of 1 July 1916. On 1 July and 11 November of each year ceremonies are held at the Thiepval Memorial. The centre – which has free entry – is open every day from 9.30am to 6.00pm, 1 March to 31 October, and 9.30am to 5.00pm, 1 November to the end of February. Annual closing is two weeks prior to and after Christmas, although there is free access to the memorial all year round. The centre has toilets and a good bookshop. You can either walk through the centre or along the public access road to reach the impressive **Thiepval Memorial** which contains the names of 73,357 names of men who have no known graves

The Thiepval Memorial Visitor Centre.

and were killed between the arrival of British units in 1915 and the retirement of the Germans to the Hindenburg Line in 1917. Designed by Sir Edwin Lutyens and constructed between 1929 and 1931, the 45m-high memorial dominates the skyline for miles around. Officially inaugurated by the Prince of Wales in 1932, it is the largest British

The Thiepval Memorial to the Missing.

memorial to the missing in the world. The red facing bricks you see are third generation and are Nori bricks from Accrington in Lancashire.

Behind the memorial is the **Thiepval Anglo-French Cemetery** symbolizing the joint efforts of the two countries in defeating the Germans during the First World War. Of the 300 British and Commonwealth casualties buried here only 61 are identified and of these, 3 were killed during the 1 July attacks. Of the 300 French burials only 47 are identified and it may have been with this sobering thought in mind that the inscription at the base of the Cross of Sacrifice was chosen: 'That the world may remember the common sacrifice of two and a half million dead, here have been laid side by side soldiers of France and of the British Empire in eternal comradeship.'

From the memorial return to your vehicle in the car park and turn left downhill to Authuille to arrive at the village war memorial where you can park. The village was held by British troops from mid-1915 – many trench names from this time have a Scottish connection due to the 51st Highland Division's tenure of the sector – until March 1918 when it was temporarily lost to advancing German forces until recovered again in July 1918. The village war memorial includes the name of **Boromée Vaquette**, who was accidentally shot by French troops near the Leipzig

Authuille village war memorial and the WFA Memorial to the Lancashire Fusiliers.

Salient, some 850m or so up the Rue Bustière, east of the village, after the Germans arrived in the area on 27 September 1914. (You will find the Vaquette family plot in the communal cemetery on the Rue d'Albert to the right of the entrance.) The small brick-built memorial to the **Lancashire Fusiliers** was erected by the Lancashire and Cheshire Branch of the Western Front Association in July 1995 and across the road you will find a memorial seat gifted to the village by the City of Glasgow in March 2003.

Continue to the church. To the left of the church entrance is a memorial plaque to the three Glasgow 'Pals' battalions – 15/, 16/ and 17/Highland Light Infantry – that fought at Thiepval on 1 July and on the right is the new bench dedicated to the memory of 16/Northumberland Fusiliers. A further 140m along the road you will find the grass track on the right leading to **Authuille Military Cemetery**, which was used from August 1915 to December 1916, and later by Indian Labour Companies. There are now over 450 buried here and of these nearly 40 are unidentified. It lies at the northern end of the **Black Horse Shelters**, which were situated 150m south of Authuille where the sloping ground sheltered the troops from German observation. Dugouts were in evidence here from early 1916 and the shelters became the HQ of the 32nd Division

The bench outside Authuille village church dedicated to the 16th Northumberland Fusiliers.

Authuille Military Cemetery.

and 90 Field Ambulance. **Charles Douie**, a subaltern serving with 1/Dorsets, took welcome respite here in 1916, recalling a 'high bank, honeycombed by dugouts and a long causeway across the marshes known as Black Horse Bridge'. The 15/Highland Light Infantry historian described them as 'a large number of cave-like dwellings let into the hillside. There were three tiers of them, and at the foot lay a roadway.'

Set on a slope with the headstones curving along the contours, the cemetery is one of the most attractive in the Ancre valley. At the bottom of the slope is a row of thirteen men of 1/Dorsets who all died on 8 May 1916 during a raid on Hammerhead Sap. Amongst those taken prisoner were **Corporal William Millar** (D.57) and 19-year-old **Second Lieutenant Vere Bayly** (A.13) who turned on their captors near the German wire enabling many of their comrades to escape back to their own lines. Bayly and Millar were killed but their bodies were recovered to be buried here along with their comrades. Charles Douie also mentions the grave of 27-year-old **Second Lieutenant Michael Armstrong** (D.69), a Royal Engineers officer from 150/Field Company who was killed in April 1916. 'The grave of an English officer was inscribed with the words "So long!" I wondered whether these were the last words of the officer or words written by one of his comrades who expected to see him again.'

Return to your vehicle and continue straight on, round the left-hand bend, to re-join the D151. This may be a good opportunity to visit Blighty Valley Cemetery which is 1km further down the D151. To reach it turn right and continue along the road until you see a CWGC signpost directing you to the cemetery. The 260m approach path is unsuitable for vehicles so ensure you pull off the road. **Blighty Valley Cemetery** is located in the particularly attractive Vallée du Hem and was begun in July 1916 and used until the following November. At the Armistice it contained 212 graves but was then greatly enlarged when 784 graves were brought in from the battlefields and small cemeteries to the east. Dug into the bank on the north side of the cemetery was 70 Brigade HQ. Most of these concentrated graves were of men who died on 1 July 1916. The cemetery now contains 1,027 casualties, 536 of which are unidentified and of these 227 are identified casualties from 1 July 1916. The cemetery is probably more associated with the 70 Brigade battalions who attacked east of Authuille Wood and many of these men were brought in after the ground was cleared. One of these is **Lieutenant Colonel Bertram Maddison** (I.B.5)

Blighty Valley Cemetery.

who was killed whilst in command of 8/York and Lancs (see **Route 7**). His adjutant, 22-year-old **Lieutenant Sydney Dawson** (V.C.36), also has his name commemorated on the Leeds University Roll of Honour. **Captain Olaf Cuthbert** (V.C.5) was a company commander in the 8/York and Lancs who, after being educated at Dover College and St John's College, Oxford, was commissioned into the battalion in October 1914. A year later he married the 20-year-old Millicent Down, whose father and uncle were partners in the local solicitors in Dorking. He was hit by machine-gun fire near Avallon Trench 10 minutes after leaving the British front line and died, aged 25. Serving with 8/KOYLI, 22-year-old **Lieutenant Marmaduke Morley** (V.J.22) arrived in France in October 1915. The former Winchester College schoolboy attacked with his battalion north of Ovillers and although twice wounded, reportedly made it across no-man's-land into the German trenches where he lost his life. Killed near Thiepval on 14 July 1916, 42-year-old **Regimental Sergeant Major William Fear** (I.A.6) of 1/8 West Yorks had already served for twenty-three years in the army, fourteen of which had been abroad with 1/West Yorks. In 1909 he was transferred from India to the Leeds Rifles

Lieutenant Marmaduke Morley.

and subsequently appointed instructor to the Leeds University OTC until he joined the 1/8 West Yorks as RSM. His Military Cross, which was awarded shortly before his death, was presented to his wife, Alice, in Leeds. Finally, you will find 21-year-old **Private Charles 'Charlie' Broadhead** (IV.G.5) of 9/York and Lancs near the Stone of Remembrance. Enlisting in Sheffield on 27 August 1914, he served in Gallipoli during 1915 where he was wounded. Returning to service, he was posted to the 9th Battalion and was killed on 1 July. Charlie was the eldest of five siblings and prior to enlisting worked as a general labourer.

Regimental Sergeant Major William Fear.

Retrace your route back towards the village war memorial and take the turning on the right – Rue Bustière – following the CWGC signpost for Lonsdale Cemetery. The route climbs uphill along a narrow metalled road that was known as **Campbell Avenue** and led to the British front line opposite the Leipzig Salient. After bearing right at the calvary on your left – easy to miss so drive slowly – you should be able to see the Thiepval Memorial on your left and a clump of poplar trees in the foreground. It was about here in what became no-man's-land that **Boromée Vaquette** was mistakenly shot on 27 September.

Continue until you reach the crossroads a little further on and stop, taking care not to block the road. To your left, some 140m from the road, the clump of trees marks the site of the *Granatloch* (see **Route 7** Map), which was at the tip of the **Leipzig Salient** and captured by 17/Highland Light Infantry (Glasgow Commercials) from 97 Brigade. Further north 16/Highland Light Infantry (Glasgow Boy's Brigade) were checked in no-man's-land and suffered heavy casualties. Moving up in support and leaving Authuille Wood at 8.30am, 11/Border Regiment (The Lonsdales) was hit by deadly enfilade machine-gun fire from the German strongpoint called the *Nordwerk*, around 1.7km to the southeast as the bullet flies, as they moved towards their jumping off trenches. In addition,

The clump of trees marking the position of the Granatloch.

96 Brigade also suffered badly in no-man's-land but small parties of the 15/Lancashire Fusiliers (1st Salford Pals) had managed to break through the German line and lodge themselves in Thiepval village, but despite attempts to reinforce them these men were either killed or captured. Meanwhile, 14 Brigade, which had been placed in reserve, were ordered to move forward. Their passage through Authuille Wood came under German machine-gun and artillery fire well before they began to cross no-man's-land towards the Leipzig Salient. At 8.45am 1/Dorsets were almost annihilated whilst crossing the open ground between the northern edge of Authuille Wood and the front-line trenches, only a handful of officers and men making it into the Leipzig Salient which was defended by 3 *Kompanie* IR 180. **Charles Douie** wrote that after moving forward the regiment 'came under the fire of massed machine guns before ever they reached our own front line at the edge of Authuille Wood'. The CSM of B Company was **Ernest Shephard**, who recalled being told to cross the open ground as quickly as possible: 'I went on ahead, Gray the company orderly behind, and No. 5 platoon behind him. How I got over I cannot imagine, the bullets were cracking and whizzing all around me. I got bullets through my clothing and equipment and was hit in the left side. The ground was covered in our dead and wounded men.' The Dorsets were followed by 19/Lancashire Fusiliers (3rd Salford Pals) but fewer than fifty officers and men made it to the Leipzig Salient losing 50 per cent of their strength in the process.

If you look back along the road towards Authuille the British front line crossed the road approximately 100m further back before swinging round north of **Authuille Wood** to run down into **Nab Valley**.

The 17/Highland Light Infantry attack straddled the road you are now on as they dashed across no-man's-land to storm the *Granatloch*. This was where **Sergeant James Turnbull** won his Victoria Cross by preventing the German garrison from expelling the Highlanders from the salient. However, reinforcing the besieged Highlanders proved costly as the machine guns positioned in the *Nordwerk* on the high ground opposite a small British salient called The Nab were able to fire indiscriminately on British battalions debouching from Authuille Wood. The track opposite the *Granatloch* leads down to Authuille Wood and was known as **Dumbarton Road**. On 1 July it was the scene of the horrific slaughter of 1/Dorsets – who lost over 300 officers and men – and The Lonsdales as they moved north to the *Granatloch* and came under fire from the *Nordwerk* machine guns.

The fields either side of Dumbarton Road would have been covered with dead and wounded men. A few survivors managed to reach the Leipzig Salient but the Lonsdales' casualties – 515 officers and men killed or wounded – included the commanding officer, 54-year-old **Lieutenant Colonel Percy Machell**. A surviving Lonsdales soldier wrote afterwards that 'Authuille Wood ran to a point and ended on our front line. We had barely gone another five yards when it seemed to rain bullets, it was hell let loose … How I missed being hit was a miracle as bullets were hitting every foot of ground and sending up spurts of dirt around my head.'

A little over 350m from the crossroads is the track leading down to **Lonsdale Cemetery** on the right where there is limited parking. The track is marked by a memorial to 1/Dorsets which was erected in May 2011. As you walk down the track to the cemetery cast a glance across to your left where the edge of the wood follows the line of **Tithebarn Street**, a former communication trench in the British lines from where several former support and front-line trenches remain undisturbed.

The Lonsdales were named after Hugh Lowther, the 5th Earl of Lonsdale, who raised the battalion from volunteers from Cumberland and Westmorland in September 1914. The original cemetery is now contained in Plot 1 and the vast majority of those men are casualties of 11/Border and 1/Dorsets. After the Armistice the cemetery was enlarged when casualties, almost all of 1916, were brought in from the surrounding battlefields and small burial plots nearby. The cemetery now contains 1,542 Commonwealth burials, 816 of whom are unidentified. There are sixty identified Lonsdale casualties and nine men of 1/Dorsets who died on 1 July buried here, although many others would have died of wounds later or remained unidentified and were buried as unknown soldiers. Spare a moment for **Lance Corporal John Bardgett** (I.C.5), who was formerly employed by the Appleby-in-Westmorland Corporation, and **Captain Colin Brown** (II.F.17) who were both killed in the Lonsdales' advance on 1 July. Another casualty of 1 July was **Sergeant James Turnbull** (IV.G.9) of the 15/Highland Light Infantry who was awarded a posthumous Victoria Cross for his actions during the defence of British gains in the Liepzig Salient. Before you leave, ponder a moment at the

The memorial to the 1st Dorset Regiment near the Lonsdale Cemetery.

grave of **Private Thomas Moore** (IV.M.6) who was 16 years old when he died fighting with 8/Loyal North Lancs on 28 August 1916 and is the youngest recorded casualty in the cemetery.

Leave the cemetery, continue downhill and stop at the bottom of the valley; take care here as the road is used by other traffic. You have just followed the British front line, which was to the right of the road, down into **Nab Valley** – the western end of which was also known as Blighty Valley where the eponymous cemetery is located – and moved into the III Corps area, having crossed the boundary separating the right flank of the

Sergeant James Turnbull VC.

32nd Division in X Corps and the 8th Division (**Major General Sir Havelock Hudson**) on the extreme left of III Corps. The naming of features in this area can be confusing, however, as maps from 1917 show Blighty Valley clearly marked as a continuation of Nab Valley, running across the road here to the northeast.

As the road begins to rise you will come to a track that crosses the road in front of you. **The Nab** was about 100m along the track to the right, and this is the ground over which 70 Brigade attacked the German front line. Continue uphill (see **Route 7** map) for another 500m to a junction with another track on the right and stop. The *Nordwerk* was across to your left and if you look back towards Blighty Valley you will have an idea of the view the German machine-gunners had of the British line west of the Leipzig Salient. On the left of the road is Authuille Wood, above which you can see the trees surrounding the *Granatloch*. Turning round again to face uphill you should also be able to see the **Pozières Memorial to the Missing** in front of you to the left. Continue into Ovillers-la-Boisselle, turning right at the junction, and park opposite the church.

Route 7

Ovillers-la-Boisselle

A circular tour beginning at: the church at Ovillers
Coordinates: 50°01′51.78″ N – 2°41′52.17″ E
Distance: 7.23km/4.86 miles
Suitable for: ⸸ ⯠
Grade: Easy (total ascent 76m)
Maps: IGN Série Bleue 2408O Albert and 2408E Bray sur Somme

General description and context: The 8th Division was tasked with taking the Ovillers spur, which lay north of the D929. On the left flank to the east of Authuille Wood **70 Brigade** suffered the highest losses in the division as they attacked just south of The Nab. The 8/KOYLI, 8/York and Lancs and 9/York and Lancs, following up, were unable to make progress in the face of heavy machine-gun fire from Thiepval. Both commanding officers of the York and Lancs battalions – **Lieutenant Colonels Bertram Maddison** (8/York and Lancs) and 49-year-old **Arthur Addison** (9/York and Lancs) – were killed in the assault. It was the failure of 70 Brigade to extinguish the threat of the *Nordwerk* strongpoint that contributed to the demise of the Lonsdales as they exited from Authuille Wood towards the Leipzig Salient. To the right of 70 Brigade, 2/Royal Berks and 2/Lincolns of **25 Brigade** advanced under heavy fire, as did 1/Royal Irish Rifles who were brought up in support. The Lincolns lost 471 officers and men, 40-year-old **Lieutenant Colonel Arthur Holdsworth,** commanding the Berks, died of his wounds a week later, as did 41-year-old **Lieutenant Colonel Carroll Macnamara** of the Royal Irish Rifles, who died on 16 July and was buried at Chorley Wood in Hertfordshire. Both battalions lost over half their strength.

On the right flank **23 Brigade** had the daunting task of crossing the widest stretch of no-man's-land – almost 900m at its widest point in front of 2/Middlesex – and were caught between the Ovillers and la Boisselle machine-gunners and riflemen as they traversed Mash Valley whilst trying to negotiate uncut wire entanglements up to 3ft high and 15ft deep which lay hidden in the tall grasses in no-man's-land. Yet, despite this flanking fire some 300 men from both 2/Middlesex

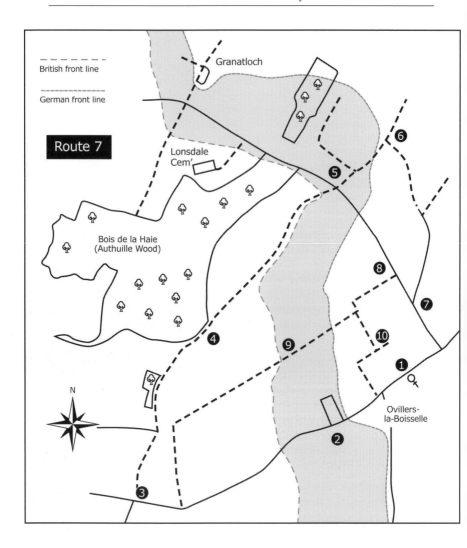

and 2/Devons did reach the German first-line trenches and held on without reinforcement until they were forced to withdraw, yet another example of the Germans' ability to prevent reserves crossing no-man's-land by putting down heavy artillery fire. Of the twenty-three officers of 2/Middlesex who took part in the attack only one returned to the British line and barely fifty NCOs and men answered their names at roll call that evening. This disaster preyed on the mind of their wounded commanding officer, 40-year-old **Lieutenant Colonel Edwin Sandys,** to such an extent that in early September 1916 he shot himself in a

London hotel and died a few days later. The village was eventually taken by the 48th Division on 16 July.

Directions to start: Ovillers-la-Boisselle is northeast of Albert and north of the D929 Albert–Pozières road. It is twinned with la Boisselle. There is plenty of parking opposite the church.

Route description: With the church ❶ on your left take the main road through the village passing the communal cemetery and **Ovillers Military Cemetery** ❷ on the right. Stop here. Built on the ground attacked by 2/Devons of 23 Brigade, the cemetery looks over Mash Valley where the 8th and 34th divisions attacked on 1 July and the ground towards la Boisselle beneath which the Y Sap mine was detonated. The cemetery was begun as a battle cemetery behind a dressing station and was used until March 1917, by which time it contained 143 graves. There are now 3,440 Commonwealth casualties buried or commemorated in the cemetery and, of these, a staggering 2,480 are unidentified. The cemetery also contains 120 French war graves from the Breton regiments which fought on the high ground to the north of Ovillers prior to the arrival of the British. There are 290 identified casualties who were killed on 1 July and no doubt many more amongst the unidentified graves. The youngest identified soldier here who was killed on that fateful morning, according to CWGC records, was 16-year-old **Rifleman Robert Power** (VII.M.5) from Waterford, who died serving with C Company, 1/RIF. Interestingly, however, he is recorded as age 13 in the Irish Census of 1911! Another youngster was 18-year-old **Private Clem Cunnington** of 8/KOYLI in 70 Brigade (I.C.2) who was killed east of Authuille Wood some 20m from the start line. His pal Ernest Deighton watched helplessly as German machine-gun bullets

The church at Ovillers-la-Boisselle.

Ovillers Military Cemetery.

scythed across his chest. Deighton was wounded in the shoulder by the same burst but survived the encounter and the war.

Of the several other notable graves in the cemetery, two casualties of 1 July are **Private George Nugent** (I.A.26A) of the 22/NF, who was reburied here on 1 July 2000 after his remains were found at the **Lochnagar Mine Crater** in October 1998, and 43-year-old Canadian-born **Lieutenant Colonel Frederick Heneker**, who commanded 21/NF and was killed on the western side of Sausage Valley. Another casualty from 103 Brigade, which attacked on the right flank of the 34th Division assault was 37-year-old **Lieutenant Colonel Louis Howard** (II.D.4) commanding the 24/NF; badly wounded on 1 July, he died the following day. Serving with 1/8 Argyll and Sutherland Highlanders, 25-year-old **Captain John Lauder** (I.A.6) was killed near Pozières three days after Christmas in 1916. The only son of the Sir Harry Lauder, the Scottish music hall and vaudeville theatre singer and comedian, it is said that his father wrote the song 'Keep Right on to the End of the Road' in the wake of John's death.

Exit the cemetery – the German front line crossed the road 70m back towards Ovillers – and turn right to continue along the road with the broad expanse of Mash Valley to the left. You will cross the site of the former British front line after 370m or so. Pause here. Imagine now the men of 2/Devons crossing the ground towards you and the cemetery beyond with 2/Middlesex on their right further down the slope, faced with the impossible task of negotiating a further 600m of no-man's-land completely exposed to concentrated German machine-gun and rifle fire in the 'killing ground' of Mash Valley. Their first wave was

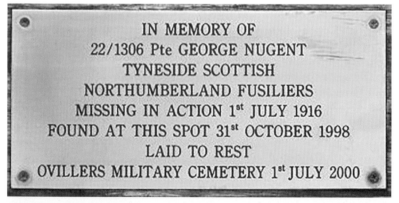

Private George Nugent's remains were discovered at Lochnagar Crater and re-buried at Ovillers Military Cemetery.

destroyed almost immediately and although later waves 'doubled' towards their objective all four waves had 'ceased to exist' long before the German line was reached by some 200 men, who were eventually forced to retire after a sharp but bloody fight.

Beyond the Middlesex right flank and crossing the boundary into the sector of the 34th Division further down into Mash Valley, 20/ and 23/NF (1st and 3rd Tyneside Scottish) of 34th Division went over north of the Albert–Bapaume Road in an effort to 'pinch out' the village and join hands behind it with others attacking from the south. Pause after a further 230m and look across towards the houses of la Boisselle lining your side of the arrow-straight D929 – the old Roman road between Albert and Bapaume – on the other side of the valley. This road was

Captain John Lauder.

the main axis of the entire British assault and so breaking the iron grip that the Germans had maintained on la Boisselle for almost two years was crucial to the success of the offensive. On your right front you will see the Aveluy–la Boisselle road heading downhill to a point where the houses thin out in the valley floor. There the German front line looped its snout just east of the twin crossroads at the southwestern end of the village to a small patch of ground dubbed the **Glory Hole** by the British, the scene of bitter fighting and almost continuous mining activity. We shall visit this area later on in **Route 8**.

Look across into the garden of the house directly opposite. This is the site of one of two large mines that were blown either side of la Boisselle to assist the Tyneside Scottish north and south of the Glory Hole in achieving their objectives unmolested. This was the Y Sap mine, blown under the eponymous sap that snaked out into no-man's-land from the line of the main road. The huge crater that resulted from the blow remained for almost fifty years, finally being filled in by 1974. If the visibility is good and the light is falling at the right angle you may just be able to make out the slightly different quality of the ground at the site.

Continue and stop at the T-junction ahead. **❸** To the left is la Boisselle – roughly halfway down that road was the site of the British-held **Keats Redan** from where 23/NF attacked – and straight ahead you can see the Basilique Notre Dame de Brebières in Albert. Turn right – going downhill on the main road – and after 300m turn right again onto a metalled track. You are now at Ovillers Post and are about to follow the route of **Ribble Street** for a short distance. Before you do, note that *Lord of the Rings* author **J.R.R. Tolkein** spent time at this spot on his way up to Hessian Trench northeast of Thiepval sometime between 17 and 20 October 1916.

Continue to the next junction of tracks – this area was known as **Donnett Post**: **Lancaster Avenue** was the track to your left and the British front line was up over the rise to your right. Note that 2/Rifle Brigade, in reserve on 1 July 1916, formed up either side of Lancaster Avenue parallel to the track you are on here before moving up communication trenches up the slope to your right towards the front line at 7.30am. It was somewhere up that slope that a British officer commissioned from the ranks and already the recipient of the VC was wounded. Blocked in due to the lack of progress of 2/Lincs and 2/Royal Berks up ahead over the ridge, the Rifle Brigade came under intense shell fire, which killed and wounded 133 officers and men, one of whom was **Second Lieutenant Harry Daniels**, who, as a Company Sergeant Major, had earned the VC for cutting a path through the German wire with Corporal Tom Noble during the Battle of Neuve Chapelle in March 1915. We tell their story in our guidebook *The Battles of French Flanders.* 'Dan VC' survived his wounds, went on to receive a Military Cross and served until 1942 – retiring as a lieutenant colonel – and died in 1953.

Continue straight ahead on the rough track past the copse towards Authuille Wood, which you can see ahead in the distance. The track brushes the southeastern corner of Authuille Wood ❹ and – in summer – makes its way under a canopy of leaves, before opening out and continuing parallel with its eastern edge. Look to your left after 250m. About 150m into the fields is the site of Quarry Post, the 9/York and Lancs battalion HQ and aid post based in a disused quarry. It was from trenches between here and the road up ahead – **Quarry Brae Street** and **Bamberidge Street** and **Liverpool Avenue** in the wood beyond – that 9/York and Lancs formed up and were thrown into battle at 8.40am. They moved diagonally across your path, up and over the higher ground to your front right, in support of the two battered assaulting battalions – 8/York and Lancs on the left and 8/KOYLI to the right.

Continue to shadow the British front line – which was up the bank to your right – and after 425m, just before the track hits the Authille–Ovillers road, you will arrive at the snout of the pronounced British salient that was The Nab. From here 8/York and Lancs went over the top across the ground to your right and were flayed by machine-gun fire from both flanks, a fate that also met the men of its sister battalion as they followed in support. 8/York and Lancs suffered almost 600 casualties, including all their officers, with almost 50 per cent of that total killed, including the CO, Lieutenant Colonel Bertram Maddison. It was the fifth highest casualty figure of any battalion involved on 1 July 1916.

The men of 9/York and Lancs also suffered. The ranks of this Kitchener battalion contained hard, uncompromising pitmen from the West Riding, with officers drawn mainly from Sheffield's professional elite: 'a rough tough lot', according to the newly commissioned Charles Carrington, who added, 'and if there are better of braver men in the world I have yet to find them'. Carrington recalled that their CO, Lieutenant Colonel Arthur Addison, was a 'pleasant, quiet regular officer, recalled from half-pay, not a dynamic man but a responsible officer with right principles …'. The battalion war diary is spare in its prose about that day and the reason becomes clear when their casualties are mentioned too: 25 officers and 736 men went into action and by 10.00pm only 180 survivors had been picked up by wagons patrolling the roads in the rear.

The story of the Pals of the York and Lancaster Regiment and their Valhalla at Serre on 1 July 1916 is almost mythological today and tends to overshadow the deeds of the regiment elsewhere on the Somme that day. However, the destruction of these two Kitchener battalions here at The Nab is a story every bit as grim and should be remembered. After the war the 9th Battalion historian ended his chapter on the Somme with a single line: 'So ended the Golden Age.'

The track meets the road up ahead where the ground opens out and there is a good view left past the end of Authille Wood back into Nab Valley and beyond up to the Thipeval spur and the Leipzig Redoubt. Lieutenant Colonel Maddison was shot down in no-man's-land somewhere here astride the road to your right. Lieutenant Colonel Arthur Addison simply disappeared. His body was not recovered for almost three months (see **Route 8**). To complete the tale of 70 Brigade's destruction – its losses, at 73 officers and 1,923 men with 2 commanding officers killed and 2 wounded, were the heaviest in the 8th Division – note that 11/Sherwood Foresters were also committed here, the men passing a continuous stream of wounded and stepping over the corpses of the 9/York and Lancs as they moved up. Many were lost well before the rest reached the British line.

At the crossroads go straight across ❺ and take the track that heads gently uphill for 350m – crossing the German fire trench – until you reach a track ❻ on the right. Turn right and stop here. You are now on the site of the German second-line trench. A few men of 8/York and Lancs reached this point and fewer still got as far as the third

Looking southwest along the track from Blighty Valley with Authuille Wood on the right.

line 150m further on. The war diary records that 'they were not seen again'. The track becomes metalled and breasts the rise at another track coming in from the left as it heads towards a water tower ahead. From this point the views west and north across the British lines in Nab Valley and up onto the Thiepval spur, topped by the Thiepval Memorial on the horizon to the north, are impressive. The *Nordwerk* strongpoint stood on the crest here some 350m due east of this point and one can appreciate how it dominated the ground all around. Unmolested by the battalions of 70 Brigade, its weapons were able to pour a withering fire into the right flank of the men crossing no-man's-land here all the way across the valley to your left and up onto the Thipeval spur beyond.

At the T-junction with the main road turn right **7** in the direction of the Thiepval Memorial and then, after 150m, turn left **8** onto a farm track for 280m to another junction where, after 50m, you turn sharp right onto a larger track heading southwest. Some 600m along this track you will find the site of Ulverston Street Trench **9** now marked by a small memorial on the right. Stop here.

At about 11.00am on 1 July 1916, about 200 men – all that remained of 2/Royal Berks – were being collected and re-grouped in trenches around this spot from where three companies of the battalion had advanced 3½ hours earlier to take the village of Ovillers behind you. They had first come under fire here at 7.15am as 2/Devons, a little further south, began to line up in front of their parapet. By the time the Royal Berks went over the Germans were alert and they were hit by intense machine-gun and rifle fire, losing just over half their strength. All except a small group on

The Ulverston Street Trench Memorial.

the extreme left, who attacked from around this spot, managed to get into the German front line but were driven out almost immediately. It was somewhere in a sap near here too that the CO, **Lieutenant Colonel Arthur Mervyn Holdsworth**, was wounded along with his second-in-command, **Major Guy Sawyer** DSO, at 7.45am. Such was the volume of fire sweeping the Berks' front-line parapet at this time that it was impossible to 'exit the trenches'. Captain Alan Hanbury-Sparrow was a 2/Royal Berks officer serving on the staff of the 8th Division HQ as forward observation officer that day and he witnessed the tragedy unfold in front of him along the front:

The view northwest of Ovillers-la-Boisselle looking across Blighty Valley and Authuille Wood to the Granatloch *and Thiepval Memorial.*

Presently, as the barrage went forward, so did the air clear, and I could see what was happening ... In no-man's-land were heaps of dead, with Germans almost standing up in their trenches, well over the top, firing and sniping at those who had taken refuge in the shell holes ... Realization came in as to what had really happened. It was the most enormous disaster that had befallen the 8th Division; the whole division was ruined.

Command of 2/Royal Berks devolved onto the acting adjutant, **Second Lieutenant Charles Mollet**, and at 11.00am Mollet was told to 'stand by' but 2/Royal Berks' part in the first day was over. Word came at 12.30pm that they were to be relieved. Lieutenant Colonel Holdsworth's wounds proved fatal and he died at Étaples on 7 July 1916. He is buried in Étaples Military Cemetery (I.A.33). Of his men, CWGC records indicate that 168 of 2/Royal Berks died in the first week of July 1916 and, if you look to the north, 102 of them who were killed on 1 July are remembered on the Thiepval Memorial you can see just 2km away. Charles Mollet survived the war with a Military Cross and bar and went on to serve in the Second World War and beyond. He retired in 1952 having served with 1st Army Supreme Headquarters Allied Expeditionary Force and HQ 15th Army Group.

Retrace your steps to the T-Junction and turn right in the direction of Ovillers and after 200m you will find the **Breton Memorial** ❿ commemorating the Bretons who fought with the 19th Regiment of

Infantry during the attack on Ovillers in December 1914. The monument, which was erected by the Breart family in 1924, is on the spot where **Augustin Breart de Boisanger**, a native of Brittany and a lieutenant in the French 19th Infantry Regiment, fell in the Battle of Ovillers-la-Boisselle on 17 December 1914. Over 800 men of the regiment – recruited almost exclusively from Brittany – were killed, wounded or taken prisoner that day, caught in the teeth of terrific rifle, machine-gun and artillery fire. This is as good a spot as any to reflect on the fact that units suffering casualties numbering in the hundreds in just a few hours, whilst attacking strong, well-defended German positions, was not an exclusively British phenomenon on the battlefields of Picardy during the First World War.

The Breton Memorial.

From the memorial follow the wide grass track round to the left and back to the main road where a left turn will take you back to your vehicle.

Ovillers-la-Boisselle to la Boisselle

Distance: 2.6km/1.6 miles
Suitable for: 🚗 🚲

From the church continue along the Rue Breart des Boisanger, named after the Breton officer whose memorial you visited in **Route 7**. Continue past the communal cemetery and **Ovillers Military Cemetery** to the T-junction. Turn left onto the D20 and descend towards la Boisselle which is directly ahead. You are now descending into the broad expanse of **Mash Valley** and after a little over 100m will cross the boundary between the 8th and 34th divisions which effectively divided the length of the valley into two. Slow down here to catch sight of the rounded Usna Hill across to the right and Mash Valley on the left where these now silent fields witnessed 2/Middlesex of 23 Brigade advance to near destruction. The point where the roadside verge on the right rises slightly is the approximate position of **Keats Redan** where the British front line joined the road from the left and followed it down towards the D929 ahead. The battalions of 102 Brigade advanced either side of Keats Redan and suffered the same fate as the men of 23 Brigade to the north.

As the road begins to level out, the approximate position of the crater made by the **Y Sap mine** – the northerly of the two large mines either side of la Boisselle due to be blown at 7.28am on 1 July 1916 – is situated in open space between the trees in the gardens of the private houses to the left. Both these large mines were planned to be 'overcharged' in order that raised lips would be thrown up metres above the surrounding ground to provide both protection from enfilade fire across no-man's-land and observation if captured, in addition to breaking the ground and destroying the strongpoints. The presence of German underground defences prevented the tunnellers of 179 Tunnelling Company from digging in a straight line to their objective so they burrowed a 475m gallery north, 23m under no-man's-land – in the fields to your left – from a point in the British line just south of where it crossed the Albert–Bapume road some 150m ahead. They then tacked right – east – for a further 475m before placing 18,415kg (40,600lb) of high-explosive ammonal in the mine chamber proper beneath Y Sap. The Germans

la Boisselle

The approximate position of the
Y Sap Crater is marked by the
depression in the fields

The D929

Mash Valley and the Y Sap crater photographed from the steps of Ovillers Military Cemetery.

appeared to have been forewarned and claimed that they had evacuated the position some time before.

At the junction with the D929 cross straight over and continue for 50m past the triangular shaped green on the right to the next junction and turn left. The church is 500m further along the road on the left.

Route 8

la Boisselle

A circular tour beginning at: the church at la Boisselle
Coordinates: 50°01′14.27″ N – 2°41′53.67″ E
Distance: 6.8km/4.2 miles
Suitable for: ⚊ 🚲
Grade: Easy (total ascent 85m)
Maps: IGN Série Bleue 2408O Albert and 2408E Bray sur Somme

General description and context: The casualties sustained on 1 July during the 34th Division's assault on la Boisselle are still remembered in the towns and villages of the northeast of England. Faced by RIR 110, the divisional commander, **Major General Edward Ingouville-Williams** – known to the troops as Inky Bill – deployed the 101 and 102 (Tyneside Scottish) brigades' battalions to attack along the two shallow valleys that ran north and south of the village, leaving 103 (Tyneside Irish) Brigade to form the third wave on the Tara and Usna ridges, a mile to the rear. This commitment of all 12 battalions to the assault undoubtedly contributed to the 6,380 casualties sustained by the division – the highest casualty figure returned by any of the attacking divisions on 1 July 1916.

Advancing north of the D929 the 102 Brigade assault across **Mash Valley,** which had 700m of no-man's-land to cross, was a total failure. Even the successful detonation of the Y Sap mine failed to impact on the carnage that was unleashed on the 20/ and 23/NF (1st and 4th Tyneside Scottish), which, in the van of the assault, were led into the attack by the skirl of the pipes played by men such as **Piper John Fellows** (20/NF) of Walker, near Newcastle. Assailed from both sides by a withering machine-gun barrage, very few men reached the German wire. Piper Fellows was hit and never seen again. He is remembered on the Thiepval Memorial. Following at 7.40am 25/NF (2nd Tyneside Irish) lost 626 officers and men killed, wounded or missing, slightly less than the 20/NF (1/Tyneside Scottish) whose casualty list amounted to 661 officers and men killed, wounded or missing, a number that included the death of their commanding officer, **Lieutenant Colonel Charles Sillery**. It was a similar story with 23/NF who attacked south of the Keats Redan. They too lost their commanding officer, **Lieutenant**

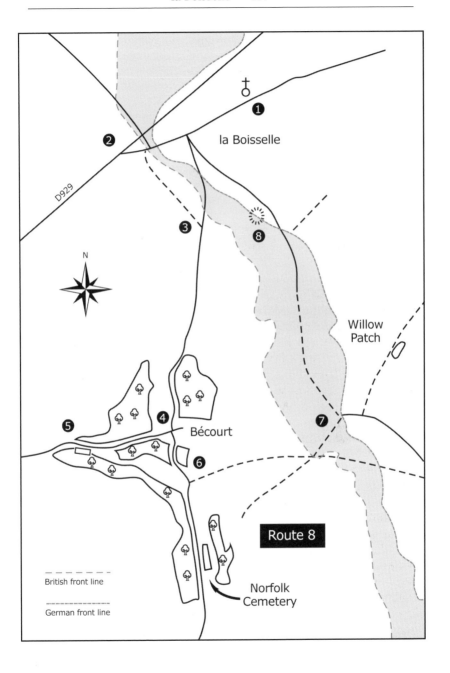

la Boisselle

D929

N

Willow
Patch

Bécourt

Route 8

British front line

German front line

Norfolk
Cemetery

Colonel William Lyle, who, according to the battalion war diary, was 'last seen alive with walking stick in hand, amongst his men about 200 yards from the German trenches'.

The 102 Brigade attack south of the village across **Sausage Valley** consisted of the 21/ and 22/NF (2nd and 3rd Tyneside Scottish), the latter piped over by **Private Alexander Findley** from High Mickley, Northumberland. Faced with a shorter advance over no-man's-land and aided no doubt by the shock of the exploding Lochnagar mine under the German *Schwaben Höhe* strongpoint, there were some initial gains as the trenches around the mine crater were overrun. Sadly, the advance was unsustainable and a combination of German counter-attacks coupled with a lack of ammunition and reinforcements forced these isolated units back towards the British line. Amongst the dead was **Lieutenant Colonel Arthur Elphinstone**, commanding 22/NF (3rd Tyneside Scottish) and Private Alexander Findley, the man who had piped his battalion into action. Both men are commemorated on the Thiepval Memorial.

Advancing on the right flank of 102 Brigade were the four battalions of 101 Brigade with 10/Lincolns (Grimsby Chums) and 15/Royal Scots (1st Edinburgh City) in the first wave followed by 11/Suffolks and 16/Royal Scots (2nd Edinburgh City or Heart of Midlothian) in the second wave. It has been claimed that a small party of 16/Royal Scots penetrated almost as far as the outskirts of Contalmaison. Gains had been made around the Lochnagar mine crater too but it had been the scene of some bitter fighting. Here a small group of 10/Lincolns 'consolidated and held positions' around the crater despite the 502 casualties reported in the battalion's war diary out of 842 officers and men who went into the attack.

Although technically in reserve, the 103 Brigade advance began almost simultaneously with the remainder of the division. With **Brigadier General Neville Cameron** wounded, the brigade's advance under the command of **Lieutenant Colonel Godfrey Steward** of 27/NF (4/Tyneside Irish) was almost doomed from the start as the battalions moved across Avoca Valley into a maelstrom of machine-gun and artillery fire. Crossing the British front line, they became entangled with struggling groups from 101 and 102 brigades, presenting an even greater target for German machine-gunners. **Sergeant John Galloway**, serving with 26/NF (3rd Tyneside Irish), remembered long lines of men being cut down by the incessant chatter of machine guns. By the time he had advanced what he felt was only a few yards most of his comrades – including himself – had been hit. On the right **Second Lieutenant George Russell** had managed to get his small party of 16/Royal Scots across four lines of trenches to the first intermediate line and beyond, halfway to Peake Woods. Here they were joined by **Second Lieutenant T. Thompson** of 24/NF and a handful of soldiers from 27/NF who represented all that remained of 103 Brigade's advance to the second objective. A few men of these two battalions of the Tyneside Irish then braced themselves again and pushed on ever deeper into German territory. In doing so they achieved an astonishing feat of endurance and persistence by advancing a remarkable total of 4km from their start line to their furthest point of penetration around Leith Fort just outside Contalmaison before being either shot down or pushed back. Thompson's commanding officer, **Lieutenant Colonel Louis Howard,** was badly wounded in the attack and died of wounds the following day.

By nightfall mixed parties of a number of battalions were holding a line centred on the strongpoint called Scots Redoubt, 750m inside the German system, and south down to Round Wood, over the boundary into the area of the 21st Division, whilst 10/Lincolns and others clung on to the area around the new mine crater. But any hopes raised by these gains were overshadowed by the catastrophic losses incurred and the fact that la Boisselle was still held by the Germans. The next day **Lieutenant Colonel Sir George McCrae** of 16/Royal Scots crossed to Scots Redoubt and, according to the divisional war diary, 'assumed command of all 34th Division troops in the German line'. He could count on just 544 men of all battalions!

It was left to the 19th Division to attack la Boisselle the next day and try to capture the village, an assault that saw three Victoria Crosses being awarded: **Lieutenant Colonel Carton de Wiart**, who was in temporary command of 57 Brigade, **Private Thomas Turrall**, of 10/Worcesters, and **Lieutenant Thomas Wilkinson**, of 7/Loyal North Lancashires, whose cross was awarded posthumously. La Boisselle was not finally cleared until 4 July 1916. It had been a desperate and bloody fight. When Lieutenant General Sir William Pulteney visited the camps of the 34th Division at Baizieux on 5 July, the three brigades were paraded individually to hear him speak – a total of 2,900 men with 102 Brigade numbering just 700 – the strength of a single battalion.

Directions to start: La Boisselle can be approached using the D929 turning off onto the D20 which continues through the village to Contalmaison. The church is on the left some 600m from the junction.

Route description: In front of the church ❶ you will find the memorial to the **19th (Western) Division** in the form of a stone cross with the divisional emblem – a butterfly – at the top. On the base are inscribed the infantry battalions and supporting units that fought with the division. The division, which had been held in reserve on 1 July, attacked la Boisselle on 2 July 1916 and finally took the village on 4 July. During the hand-to-hand fighting amongst the rubble on 3 July a line was held through the church ruins here by 10/Warwicks and 8/Gloucesters.

Leave the church and head downhill, passing the war memorial on the right and the road off to the left signed Bécordel Bécourt, to the cordoned off area of wasteland on the left. This is the **Glory Hole** – the Germans called the area the *Granathof* (shell farm) and the French had known it as the *Ilôt* (islet) – the scene of frenetic mining and counter-mining activity by both sides since before the British arrived. In places here the opposing lines were separated by as little as 30m of no-man's-land and often only

The church at la Boisselle with the 19th Division Memorial standing in front of the entrance.

by the width of the mine craters, many of which you can see overlapping here. The old village cemetery was here and was completely destroyed. It is now on the other side of the D929. Charles Douie, whom we last heard from in Authille Military Cemetery, was here in March 1916:

I learned something of the reputation of the La Boisselle trenches. They were among the most notorious in the British lines. For a considerable distance the opposing lines were divided only by the breadth of the mine craters: the British posts lay in the lips of the craters protected by thin layers of sandbags and within bombing distance of the German posts … I and a companion went forward to inspect the mine craters … East of the cemetery was the heaped white chalk of several mine craters. Above them lay the shattered tree stumps and litter of brick which had once been the village of La Boisselle. We … came to the craters, and the saps which ran between them. Here there was no trench, only sand-bags, one layer thick, and about two feet above the top of the all-prevailing mud…. We crawled away and came in time to a trench behind the cemetery, known as Gowrie Street. Liquid slime washed over and above our knees; tree trunks riven into strange shapes lay over and alongside the trench. The wintry day threw greyness over all. The shattered crosses of the cemetery lay at every angle about the torn graves, while one cross, still erect by some miracle, overlooked the craters and the ruins of La Boisselle. The trenches were alive with men, but no sign of life appeared over the surface of the ground. Even the grass was withered by the fumes of high explosive. Death indeed, was emperor here.

It takes little imagination then to understand why the British – with true gallows humour – called it the Glory Hole!

Although private property, parts of this area can be seen from the roads to the north and east. The land is tortured – heavily cratered and uneven – and provides ample physical evidence of the dark, dirty, claustrophobic and bitter underground war waged here. Over five miles of tunnels, French, British and German, dug down to a depth of 110ft emanate from the site and run under the village. From 2011–14 the La Boisselle Study Group, a team of historians, archaeologists and specialists, worked on site, opening up and exploring the British tunnel system. As part of their investigations they cleared much of the scrub that obscured the pitted nature of the ground. Now one can still see a good deal of what is actually quite a large 2-hectare site. During their surface archaeological work, the team recovered the remains of over ten British, French and German soldiers. A number of these have been identified and subsequently reburied with full military honours. The site is now managed by a local group, the Association des Amis de l'Ilot de La Boisselle.

Continue down the road – Rue de la 34e Division – to the grassed area on your right where you will find the **Tyneside Memorial Seat** situated at the junction ❷ with the D929. The seat lies almost on the British front line of 1 July and commemorates the 102 (Tyneside Scottish) and 103 (Tyneside Irish) brigades which attacked either side of the village. The memorial was erected soon after the Armistice and unveiled by Marshal Foch in April 1922. Retrace your route for approximately 80m and take the metalled road on the right opposite the triangular traffic island that runs past a private house on the right. The road – which runs parallel to the British front line across to your left – soon turns to grass and skirts the western edge of the Glory Hole then continues towards the ridge in front of you which was known as the **Chapes Spur**. Where the track joins a metalled road ❸ – Route de Bécourt – turn right. On your right is **Avoca Valley**, beyond which are the rounded shapes of **Tara Hill** on the left and **Usna Hill** to its right. At 7.35am on 1 July 1916 the men of 103 Brigade left their positions on Tara Hill to cross Avoca

The Tyneside Memorial seat at the junction with the D929.

Valley, as they reached the road you are now on many of them were cut down by German machine-gunners firing from the high ground ahead of them. On your left is **Sausage Valley** which heads northeast to skirt la Boisselle to the south.

As you top the rise, the tower of the Basilique Notre Dame de Brebières in Albert comes into view, whilst behind you is the Thiepval Memorial. Soon after the road sweeps round through **Bécourt Wood** and you arrive in the centre of the village. The chateau ❹ on your left was rebuilt after the war and now caters for groups involved with Albert's twinning programme. Prior to 1 July the building housed units of the Tyneside Scottish Brigade, although units frequently bivouacked on the hill south of Bécourt Military Cemetery. The 16/Royal Scots were billeted in Bécourt Wood prior to their attack on 1 July, and 27-year-old **Private Primrose Fairweather**, a school teacher from Leith, remembered being 'entrenched in the grounds of what was a rather handsome country house'. **Lieutenant Colonel Sir George McCrae**, commanding the battalion, claimed one of the less damaged rooms for himself and established battalion HQ in the kitchen. The village was also host to a large artillery depot and used by 14/Field Ambulance which was based here for the opening days of the Battle of the Somme. XV Corps had a walking wounded post here as well as an advanced dressing station.

Bécourt Chateau before the war.

Imagine for a moment the scene that greeted **Major Walter Vignoles**, who had been wounded in the hand whilst commanding his company of the 10/Lincolns (Grimsby Chums) in Sausage Valley. Around him were dead and dying men who had been brought in from the battlefield whilst orderlies and medical staff did their best to separate those who might live from those who would not. After some initial treatment he joined the long line of walking wounded as they made their way to Albert.

Keeping the chateau on your left, bear right along the Rue d'Albert for 450m to **Bécourt Military Cemetery**. **5** The cemetery was begun in August 1915 by the 51st (Highland) Division and there are now 713 identified casualties buried here, but only 15 are victims of 1 July 1916. However, there are many who were killed in the subsequent attacks after 1 July, such as **Lieutenant Leonard Hammond** (I.R.21) who was killed fighting with 10/Duke of Wellington's on 5 July 1916 near **Horseshoe Trench** during the 23rd Division attacks towards Contalmaison. After enlisting in the Inns of Court Officer Training Corps, he was commissioned in September 1914. His elder brother, **Major Paul Hammond**, was wounded by a stray bullet with the 8/East Lancs in February 1916 at Foncquevillers and died of pneumonia on 25 February. Killed in this same costly attack were 24-year-old **Lieutenant Adolph Lavarack** (I.R.22), a former clerk at the London Stock Exchange, and 21-year-old **Second Lieutenant Walter Taylor** (I.R.21). Also killed were **Private James Field** (I.R.24), who was born

Bécourt Military Cemetery.

in County Cork and enlisted in Barnsley, and 31-year-old **Captain Herbert Carpenter** (I.R.25), who was another member of the London Stock Exchange. One of the most senior officers buried here is 49-year-old **Lieutenant Colonel Arthur Addison** (I.W.23), who commanded 9/York and Lancs on 1 July. Like many on that fateful day his body lay where he had fallen until it was found on 23 September 1916 between Aveluy and Ovillers. It was brought back to Bécourt Wood, where his battalion was at the time and he was buried at 3.00pm two days later. Found on his body was a short diary which revealed, according to **Lieutenant Colonel Harold Farnell Watson**, the CO of 11/Sherwood Foresters, who had himself been wounded on 1 July, that 'he must have lived for at least 2 if not 3 days before he died'. The battalion history tells that the final words scribbled in the diary as Addison lay dying were 'tell the Regiment I hope they did well'. The inscription on his grave – *Quis separabit* (Who will separate us?) – is that of the Royal Irish Rifles, his old regiment, and perhaps the enduring hope of his wife Mildred.

Killed on 24 January 1916 was the soldier-poet 25-year-old **Second Lieutenant Hugh 'Rex' Freston** (I.E.16). Serving with 6/Royal Berks, he joined his battalion four days before Christmas 1915 and his war lasted barely a month before his death. Two of his better known poems are 'The March' and 'Going into Action'. Before you leave, find the headstone of 20-year-old **Bombardier Thomas Luke** from Queen's Park, London. His headstone (Sp Mem 1) stands alone behind the Stone of Remembrance. He was killed serving with B Battery, 95 Artillery Brigade on 24 June 1916.

You now have a choice of routes. You can either retrace your steps to the three-way junction by the chateau and bear round to the right on the Rue de Château – take care here if you are on a bike as the road is quite steep as it swings round to the left – and at the bottom of the hill take the left-hand fork to find a calvary ❻ on the left. Or, use the grass track that can be accessed at the top of the cemetery behind the Cross of Sacrifice. The track descends through the Bois de la Hayere and meets the road about 150m south of the calvary. Turn left to the calvary. The calvary – set back in the trees and easy to miss when the vegetation is at its thickest during the summer – is dedicated to the memory of **Lieutenant Joseph de Valicourt**, whose parents once lived at Bécourt Chateau and who was killed fighting on the Aisne in 1917.

Keep the calvary to your left and take the track ahead which rises immediately. The boundary between the 34th and 21st divisions ran northeast, following the eastern edge of the tree line – which you will pass in 50m on the left – before curving gently east to follow the floor of Sausage Valley towards the British front line. Ignoring the first track on the left, continue uphill until the views become much clearer. To your left is Bécourt Wood where much of the chalk spoil from the huge **Lochnagar Mine** ❽ was disposed of, whilst across to the right you should be able to see the spire of Fricourt church and the wooded expanse of **Bois Français**, which we visit in **Route 9**. At the top of the hill is a single tree marking a crossroads of tracks on the site of the former British front line. Bear left here towards the clump of trees in the distance. This is the **Willow Patch**, or Bois de Bécordel, as it is known today. Beyond the Willow Patch – 500m to the north – is the approximate position of **Scots Redoubt**, which was held so tenaciously during 1 July

The calvary dedicated to the memory of Lieutenant Joseph de Valicourt.

1916 by 16/Royal Scots and a mixed force made up of two officers and about eighty-five men from 15/Royal Scots and six officers and sixty men from the Lincolns, Suffolks and Northumberland Fusiliers. After dark on 1 July the small force was strengthened as it was joined by other groups that had survived the day's fighting and was re-supplied by others crossing no-man's-land. These included **Lieutenant Colonel Sir George McCrae,** who organized the defence of Scots redoubt and the surrounding trenches before his command was relieved by units of the 23rd Division on 3 July and found its way back to British lines. The 56-year-old McCrae was reported by 16/Royal Scots historian Jack Alexander to have 'grown a stubbly white beard and resembled nothing so much as a poorly dressed scarecrow. There was blood on his tunic and his face was streaked with dirt.'

Lieutenant Colonel Sir George McCrae.

At the next junction ❼ of tracks stop. You will be turning left now but before you do, consider that you have just traversed the 280m width of no-man's-land and are now on the German front line which came south, roughly from the direction of the Willow Patch, to this point before curving away to the southeast towards Fricourt. The British front line ran north from the tree you have just come from, along the slopes to the west and crossed the track 400m to your left before meandering along its route down through **Sausage Valley** towards the Lochnagar mine crater, the vegetation surrounding which you should be able to make out, hard by the left of the track on the other side of the valley, about 1km distant.

Before continuing down into the valley, stop and look along the line of the track ahead of you. On 1 July the British front line running to the left of the track would have been packed with men waiting for the final artillery and mortar barrage to cease before they went 'over the top' and crossed the ground towards the German front line. **Private Frank Scott**, advancing with 16/Royal Scots across the near shoulder of the Chapes Spur you can see on the other side of Sausage valley, recalled:

It was pure hell crossing that ground, owing to their machine guns and shell fire. It was awful seeing all your chums go under and not

The track crosses Sausage Valley before rising to the site of the Lochnagar mine crater just above the centre of the image.

being able to do anything for them. Some of us managed to get over all right and found their front line absolutely battered to bits, practically just chalk heaps and hardly anybody in it.

Continue down into Sausage Valley and as you pass a track on the right glance across to see **Gordon Dump Cemetery**, which we visit later.

The **Lochnagar mine crater** ❽ is now on your left, just past the new car park area and is one of several visible along the Western Front today. Lochnagar crater is now owned by Richard Dunning, who, in 1978, purchased the land to ensure it could be maintained as a permanent memorial. The crater's name derives from a nearby communication trench – **Lochnagar Street** – in which the shaft was located. It was formed when a combined total of 60,000lb of ammonal – stacked in two chambers 18m apart – was detonated under a German position known as the *Schwaben Höhe* at 7.28am, 2 minutes before zero, on 1 July. Like the mine at Y Sap, the Lochnagar mine was overcharged – 16,330kg (36,000lb) in one chamber and 10,886kg (24,000lb) in the other – in order to produce a wide, raised lip that would provide some cover from enfilade machine-gun fire for the attacking battalions of 10/Lincolns and

The Lochnagar mine crater today.

11/Suffolks. The explosion blew at least half of 7 *Kompanie*, RIR 110 to oblivion – and the body parts undoubtedly lie within the crater today, but there is little doubt that British infantry were caught by the debris of the initial blast. The explosion was observed by **Second Lieutenant Cecil Lewis** of 3 Squadron RFC who was overhead at the time and his machine was buffeted by the updraught:

> The whole earth heaved and flashed, a tremendous and magnificent column rose up into the sky. There was an ear-splitting roar, drowning all the guns, flinging the machine sideways in the repercussing air. The earth column rose higher and higher almost to 4,000 feet. There it hung, or seemed to hang, for a moment in the air, like the silhouette of some great cypress tree, then fell away in a widening cone of dust and debris.

There is a large wooden cross made from English oak which was erected beside the crater in 2011. It is the second to be erected on the site after the original – put up in 1986 and made from the roof timbers of a deconsecrated church near Durham – blew down after twenty-four years. Other memorials around the crater can be accessed via the duckboard pathway which carries a number of brass memorial plaques.

Second Lieutenant Cecil Lewis.

Leave the crater and turn left towards the T-junction with the Albert–Pozières road to cross the ground over which the 21, 22 and 26/NF attacked – from left to right – the Shwaben Höhe. Glance left just after house on the corner of the road from Bécourt that comes in steeply from your left and you will see another view of the Glory Hole. At the junction ahead you will see the **Old Blighty Tea Rooms** opposite. At the time of writing opening times are 10.30am to 5.00pm, Thursday to Monday, whilst Tuesdays and Wednesday are by appointment only; email: old_blighty@hotmail.com.

Turn right at the junction to return to your vehicle. This is a good opportunity to visit the **34th Division Memorial**, the pathway to which you will find 200m further up the road on the left marked by a rectangular shaped building with a green metal door. Take care here as the narrow entrance to the memorial is easy to miss. A grass path leads to the memorial overlooking Mash Valley and Ovillers Military Cemetery. It was unveiled in May 1923 by **Major General Sir Cecil Nicholson**, who commanded the division after Major General Ingouville Williams was killed on 22 July 1916.

The memorial to Private Tom Easton at Lochnagar.

A number of brass plaques are set into the walkway that surrounds the crater. These three commemorate the three VC winners associated with the area.

The 34th Division Memorial which overlooks Mash Valley.

To find **Gordon Dump Cemetery** continue uphill on the D20 past the 34th Division Memorial for some 700m until a CWGC signpost on the right directs you along a grass pathway to the cemetery. There is parking at the cemetery. Should you wish to visit the **16/Royal Scots Memorial** continue into Contalmaison and turn right at the obvious junction. The memorial is next to the church and was erected in 2004. The battalion had strong links with Heart of Midlothian Football Club and Raith Rovers. Many supporters of Hearts also joined up, as did fans of Hibernian, the other main Edinburgh football club. But it was Hearts that the battalion was most closely associated with, and a smaller plaque on the memorial is in memory of the 'players, ticket-holders and supporters of Heart of Midlothian Football Club' who advanced on Contalmaison on 1 July 1916. Close by is a bas-relief showing the advances made by the battalion that day. To find the **Bell's Redoubt** Memorial continue past the church for 150m and take the turning on the left – Rue de Mametz – the memorial is approximately 50m further on the left and was dedicated in July 2000.

Bell's Redoubt Memorial at Contalmaison.

Gordon Dump Cemetery was begun by fighting units after 10 July 1916 when it was called Gordon Dump Cemetery or Sausage Valley Cemetery and was closed to burials in September 1916 when it contained the graves of ninety-five soldiers, mainly Australians. The remainder of the cemetery was formed after the Armistice when graves were brought in from the surrounding 1916 battlefields. There are now 1,676 casualties buried here of which a staggering 1,053 are unidentified. Possibly the most well-known individual is **Second Lieutenant Donald Bell** (IV.A.8) from Harrogate, who was the only professional footballer to receive the Victoria Cross and was 25 years old when he was killed on 10 July 1916 serving with the 9/Yorkshire Regiment (The Green Howards). Supported by Corporal Colwill and Private Batey, he knocked out a machine-gun position near **Horseshoe Trench** – later renamed **Bell's Redoubt** – but was killed five days later. His award was announced in September 1916. In November 2010 the Bell VC group was bought by the Professional Footballer's Association for a hammer price of £210,000.

The imposing memorial to the 15th and 16th Royal Scots at Contalmaison.

Of the 310 identified casualties of the 1 July attacks forty-one are from the 15/ and 16/Royal Scots who attacked south of the Lochnagar mine crater. Of the men of McCrae's 16/Royal Scots, **Lance Sergeant David Smart** (VII.I.6) was caught by machine-gun fire from the lip of the Lochnagar crater and died alongside **Private Primrose Fairweather**. **Private George Cockburn** (IV.R.3) stumbled across his brother, Peter Cockburn, lying with a wound to his chest south of Sausage Redoubt. After attending to his wounded brother he continued with the advance, turning only to shout 'We've got them on the run.' That was the last time Peter saw his brother, he was killed sometime later. **Captain Lionel Coles** (V.E.5) was commanding C Company when he was killed – aged 27 – at about 11.00am near Sausage Redoubt. His servant, **Private John Bird**, was killed as he rushed to assist him. Bird's name is on the Thiepval Memorial. Another casualty of 1 July was 35-year-old **Private John Coddington** (VI.6.10) of the Grimsby Chums who was Major Walter Vignoles' servant. Recovering from his wound in Wandsworth hospital, Vignoles asked his wife to ensure Annie Coddington and her four children were not experiencing financial hardship.

Front Line Spine Route
la Boisselle to Fricourt

Distance: 7.5km/4.6 miles
Suitable for: 🚗 🚴

This section of the front line spine route follows the first part of **Route 8** (see map) to Bécourt after which it continues south visiting Norfolk Cemetery and Dartmoor Cemetery before arriving at Fricourt. From the church at la Boisselle continue downhill and turn left at the Old Blighty Tea Rooms following signs for the C9 to Bécourt and *'La Grande Mine'*. Take the right fork to Bécourt after 70m and after a further 450m you will pass the track on the right leading back to the Glory Hole which you came up on **Route 8**. You are now travelling down the Route de Bécourt with Sausage Valley on your left and Avoca Valley on the right, which you will also recognize.

Continue into Bécourt and stop briefly by the chateau. If you have not already visited **Bécourt Military Cemetery** you can now do so by turning right along the Rue d'Albert. (A full description of Bécourt and the cemetery can be found in **Route 8**.) Return to the village centre and continue downhill for some 280m noting the calvary on the left.

Continue straight ahead and, as you round the bend, the Cross of Sacrifice at **Norfolk Cemetery** should be visible on the left. There is limited parking opposite. The cemetery was begun by 1/Norfolks in August 1915 and 16-year-old **Private Issac Laud** (I.A.11), who died on 9 August 1915, was one of the first casualties buried here. By 1918 there were around 280 graves, with a further 268 graves brought in from surrounding battlefields. Situated in a long valley, numerous artillery batteries – including 95 Brigade RFA – were located here during the 1 July battle. Possibly the most well-known individual is 36-year-old **Major Stewart Loudoun-Shand** (I.C.77), a former tea merchant in Ceylon, now Sri Lanka, who was awarded the Victoria Cross – the first to a soldier of the New Army 21st Division – at Fricourt on 1 July when B Company of 10/Yorkshire Regiment struggled to get over the top in the face of fierce German machine-gun fire which ripped across their parapets. Loudoun-Shand immediately leapt on to the parapet, helped the men out, up and over it and encouraged them in every way until he was mortally wounded. Even then, he insisted on being propped up in the trench and went on encouraging his men until his life ebbed away. The twenty-six identified men recorded as being killed on 1 July are mainly concentrated in Plots I and II with 35-year-old **Lieutenant Colonel Colmar Lynch** DSO (I.B.87), of 9/KOYLI, being the most senior. He was killed close to **South Sausage Support Trench**, near the Willow Patch, whilst attacking with the 21st Division. Close by is 24-year-old **Captain Gordon Haswell** (I.B.92) of the same battalion who joined the staff of Harrow County School in August 1913 to teach English and history. His younger brother, 19-year-old Lieutenant Frederick Haswell, serving with 2/East Yorks, was killed on 23 April 1915. The third 9/KOYLI officer killed on 1 July was **Captain William Walker** (I.B.91) who brought

Major Stewart Loudoun-Shand VC.

the total officer casualties sustained by the battalion to thirteen killed and nine wounded, of whom two later died of wounds. Two men who were shot for desertion on 26 June 1916 were 'old sweats' **Private John Jennings** (I.D.85) and **Private Griffith Lewis** (I.D.86), both of 2/South Lancs and who had been on the run since October 1915. They were eventually picked up in May 1916 in London in Britain, shipped to France and executed.

Leave the cemetery and continue along the valley passing under the D939 to a T-junction. Turn right to **Dartmoor Cemetery**, the entrance to which you will find opposite the communal cemetery. There are only six unidentified casualties amongst the 768 burials in the cemetery which was begun by British troops in August 1915 and known as Bécordel-Bécourt Military Cemetery. At the request of the 8/ and 9/Devons its name was changed in May 1916 to Dartmoor Cemetery. Several graves of note are to be found here, one of which is 30-year-old **Lieutenant Colonel Harry Allardice** (I.F.42), who was killed on 1 July commanding 13/NF to the north of Fricourt. After leaving Eton and Sandhurst, he was commissioned in 1907 into 36/Jacob's Horse becoming adjutant in 1914. The regimental badge on his headstone is that of Jacob's Horse. Look out for 67-year-old **Lieutenant Henry Webber** (I.E.54), who died of wounds received in **Mametz Wood** on 21 July 1916. He was one of the oldest officers killed whilst serving on the Western Front as Transport

Dartmoor Cemetery.

Officer with 7/South Lancs. Two rows behind is the grave of 26-year-old **Private James Miller** (I.C.64), whose award of the Victoria Cross was gazetted in September 1916. A battalion runner with 7/King's Own, Miller was shot through the back whilst crossing open ground and, despite his wounds, he delivered his message and died soon afterwards. Spare a moment for two soldiers who were father and son and who were both killed on 5 September 1916 serving with A Battery, 156 Artillery Brigade – 44-year-old **Sergeant George Lee** (I.A.35) is buried next to his son, 19-year-old **Corporal Robert Lee** (I.A.36).

Leave the cemetery and turn right on the Rue du Pont to reach the main road ahead and turn right towards Fricourt. After just over a kilometre take the left turn into Fricourt – signposted D147 – passing **Fricourt British Cemetery (Bray Road)** on your left, which we will visit later during **Route 9.** Continue to the centre of the village and park near the war memorial.

Route 9

Fricourt

A circular tour beginning at: Fricourt village war memorial
Coordinates: 49°59′49.36″ N – 2°42′48.86″ E
Distance: 7.2km/4.8 miles
Suitable for: ♦ ♻
Grade: Moderate (total ascent 114m)
Maps: IGN Série Bleue 2408E Bray sur Somme

General description and context: This route crosses the ground over which the 21st Division assault on Fricourt took place and touches on the 7th Division assault on the Bois Français trenches. Apart from a visit to the German Cemetery north of Fricourt, we visit four other CWGC cemeteries and one communal cemetery. Fricourt, adopted by Ipswich after the war, was located at the southwestern point of the entire length of the British front line in the angle of what resembled a giant capital letter 'L' leaning slightly backwards. It was the only place on the right wing of the 1 July attacks – along the horizontal leg of the 'L' – where the British failed to achieve their first-day objectives. As with Gommecourt, and la Boisselle, the village was assaulted from north and south – mines were also to be used opposite a small British salient called **The Tambour** – in the hope that its encirclement would lead to the surrender of the German garrison. With the **Willow Stream** acting as the divisional boundary, the 21st Division (**Major General David 'Soarer' Campbell**) was ranged along the western slopes of the Fricourt Spur, whilst the 7th Division (**Major General Herbert Watts**) was further south, facing north opposite Mametz.

Fricourt itself was heavily defended by RIR 111 and two support lines stiffened its defence still further, which accounts for the reluctance of the British to attack frontally. On the 7th Divisional front were 20/Manchesters and 1/Royal Welch Fusiliers from 22 Brigade, whilst further round to the northwest were the four battalions from 50 Brigade – which were attached to 21st Division. The line between the communal cemetery and The Tambour was held by 7/Yorkshire Regiment (Green Howards), whilst 10/West Yorkshire Regiment's sector ran from The Tambour to a small salient named **Purfleet,** northwest of **Red Cottage**,

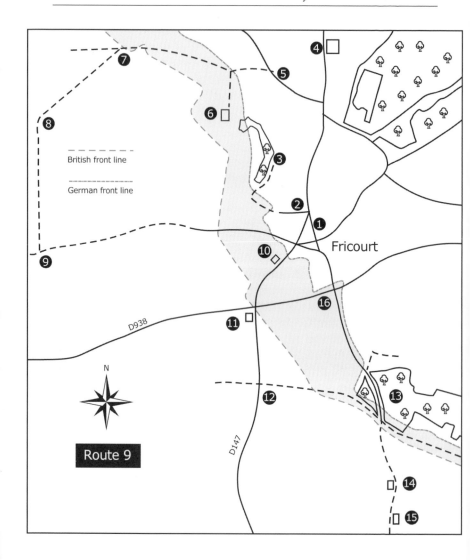

which was behind German lines to the north of the village. In support were 7/East Yorks and 6/Dorsets in and around Bécordel-Bécourt.

The British attack began 2 minutes after The Tambour mines were detonated. Three large mines had been prepared by 178 Tunnelling Company with the intention of forming craters which would shield the attacking infantry from enfilade fire. However, only two of the three exploded – water flooded the chamber of the largest charge and the other two, 'under charged', failed to create the high rims to protect the assaulting troops. It didn't matter in any case: as was so often the case in the First World War, the German infantrymen proved adept at rushing freshly blown craters and quickly established themselves on the torn ground before the British arrived, in circumstances similar to those that were even then playing out on the Hawthorn Ridge above Beaumont Hamel (see **Route 5**).

North of 50 Brigade the battalions of 63 and 64 brigades completed the left flank of 21st Division. Attacking across the ground south of the Willow Patch towards **Crucifix Trench** and **Shelter Wood**, 64 Brigade had consolidated positions east of the D147 Contalmaison road by nightfall. It was in this area during the afternoon of 1 July that **Major Stewart Loudoun-Shand** performed the actions that were to lead to the award of the Victoria Cross. Like the 64 Brigade attack, that of 63 Brigade was also partially successful. Having attacked **Empress Trench**, 8/Somerset Light Infantry managed to advance to the Contalmaison road with heavy casualties, but on their right 4/Middlesex were subjected to a barrage of machine-gun fire and only a handful were able to consolidate a new line north of Fricourt under their commanding officer, **Lieutenant Colonel Henry Bicknell**.

The 50 Brigade attack was an unmitigated disaster: 10/West Yorks – a Kitchener battalion formed at York in early September 1914 – sustained the highest casualty figures of any attacking battalion on 1 July, whilst 7/Green Howards – who attacked north of **Wing Corner –** were also cut down in no-man's-land. Within 3 minutes the latter had lost 351 officers and men. A similar fate befell 7/East Yorks where the two leading companies were unable to make headway losing 155 officers and men. On the right 20/Manchesters had the longest frontage allocated to any of the assaulting battalions on 1 July, a sector that ran from the communal cemetery along **Aeroplane Trench** to the small quarry east of **Bois Français**. Their advance began at 2.30pm and almost immediately they came under fire from the RIR 109 machine guns at Wing Corner. The leading companies crossed no-man's-land, but the attack faltered on the German support lines. The battalion's commanding officer, **Lieutenant Colonel Harold Lewis**, was one of the 325 officers and men killed and wounded.

Directions to start: Fricourt can be approached from Albert in the west along the D938 or from the east along the D64. The war memorial is close to Fricourt Military Cemetery (Bray Road) on the D147.

Route description: With the war memorial ❶ behind you head uphill on the Rue d'Arras and take the first turning on the left ❷ along a narrow track running between house number 11 and a large agricultural shed. This track leads to the site of **The Tambour mine craters** ❸ now on private property but it is possible to view the site through the trees and undergrowth. The width of no-man's-land at this point was some 140m and apart from the main mine craters there are numerous others, bearing testament to the underground war that was waged in this sector prior to July 1916.

Retrace your steps to the Rue d'Arras and turn left, passing the Rue de la Boisselle on your left. The small stand of trees on the right was known as **Lonely Copse.** The sombre **Fricourt German Cemetery** ❹ is on the right and if you stand on the raised bank near the northernmost entrance you can look out over the ground attacked by the battalions of 63 and 64 brigades. A visit to this cemetery is a must on anyone's itinerary if they are to understand the huge loss of life that took place on all sides during the conflict. There are 17,027 German soldiers interred here and its size reflects the reluctance on the part of the French to provide space for the burial of German dead in numerous cemteries. A total of 11,970 men are buried in 4 mass graves, known as *Gemeinschaftsgräber*, with 5,331 commemorated by name whilst the remainder are unknown. The metal crosses were installed in 1977 when the cemetery underwent

The Tambour mine craters.

The German Military Cemetery at Fricourt.

a major renovation but it still remains almost impossible to link names to regiments or particular actions. However, a closer inspection reveals a large number of men from RIR 8 who defended Thiepval in July 1916. This is the site in which *Rittmeister* **Manfred von Richthofen** was buried in 1920 for the second time – the first being at Bertangles in 1918 – before his body was taken back to Germany in 1925.

Retrace your route for 320m to the Rue de la Boisselle and turn right past private houses – following the CWGC signpost for Fricourt New Military Cemetery. The houses on the left are on the former site of **Red Cottage**, a significant German support position. Bear left at the fork in the track ❺ from where you should be able to see the **Willow Patch** (see **Route 8**) across to the right, whilst the trees on your left mark the site of The Tambour mine craters. As you continue along the track the Cross of Sacrifice marking **Fricourt New Military Cemetery** ❻ appears on your left and can be accessed by the grass path. Constructed in what was no-man's-land, the cemetery is essentially the graveyard of 10/West Yorks who were buried in four mass graves after the capture of Fricourt on 2 July, several of the headstones recording the names of two or more soldiers. Of the 210 casualties buried here 159 are those of 10/West Yorks and 38 are those of 7/East Yorks who attacked across the same ground with two companies at 2.33pm. Buried here is the West Yorks commanding officer, 41-year-old **Lieutenant Colonel Arthur Dickson** (C.12), who died of wounds on 1 July leading his battalion across the ground north of The Tambour Salient. Next to him is 22-year-old **Lieutenant John Shann** (C.13), the battalion's adjutant, who, after leaving Leeds Grammar School, won a place at Oxford as an exhibitioner in 1913. One of the lesser known soldier poets, 29-year-old **Lieutenant Alfred Victor Ratcliffe** (C.8), was training to be a barrister before he was commissioned in 1914. A graduate of Sidney Sussex College, Cambridge, Ratcliffe's parents placed a private memorial by his headstone which is still in position today. Ratcliffe's words from the final stanza of his poem 'Optimism' seem appropriate when standing at his grave:

> For tiny hopes like tiny flowers of Spring
> Will come, though death and ruin hold the land …

A graduate of King's College, London, 28-year-old **Lieutenant Humphrey Allen** (C.11) worked in the Malay States before arriving in France in July 1915. Canadian national 23-year-old **Captain Archibald 'Archie' Anderson** (C.2) was killed advancing with C Company. Hailing from Winnipeg, he was a law student before being commissioned in 1914. Seven years his junior, according to CWGC records, was Hull-born **Private Albert Barker** (B.3) of 7/East Yorks, who was the youngest soldier known to die on the Somme battlefront on 1 July. In April 1901, however, Albert was recorded as age 1 and ten years later, in April 1911, he was 12, making him 17 on 1 July 1916! Spare a thought for 18-year-old **Private Frank Smith** of 10/West Yorks (D.2), who lived in Leeds with his mother and stepfather and delivered milk from the local dairy.

Retrace your steps to the track and stop. This may be a good moment to consider the attack of 63 Brigade and that of 10/West Yorks which took place north of The Tambour, marked by the trees and shrubs across to your left. In the belief that the mine craters would protect their right flank the West Yorks made their attack at 7.30am just north of The Tambour across this very ground. The attack was timed to coincide with that of 4/Middlesex to form a defensive flank on the left of 63 Brigade. Until fairly recently it was widely believed that many of the West Yorks were cut down by a solitary machine gun positioned opposite the northern end of The Tambour. However, it looks increasingly likely that it was a single machine gun situated at the southern end that wreaked so much havoc on the West Yorkshiremen and those of 7/Yorkshire

Regiment who were attacking across the Vallée Reynard towards the German-held **Fricourt Trench**.

As most of the West Yorks were systematically shot down together with Lieutenant Colonel Dickson, his second-in-command and battalion adjutant, small groups of survivors miraculously reached the German front line unscathed passing along **Red Lane Trench** to Red Cottage, which you passed on the way to the cemetery. One group of West Yorks under **Lieutenant Philip Howe** – whom one of the authors interviewed in his home in the Peak District of Derbyshire in the early 1980s – reached the area of **Lonely Lane** communication trench and **Lonely Trench**, the fourth German line, which ran west of and parallel to the Contalmaison road, just 50m or so on the opposite side from the entrance to the German cemetery where you were earlier. Howe had been in the first wave, a fact he always put down to his survival. Turning round expecting to see the bulk of his battalion behind him, Howe – a Sheffield-born solicitor's clerk – was amazed to find he had just twenty men. The name of the trench they had reached

Captain Archibald Anderson.

seemed particularly apposite. Howe was shot in the hand here and lost consciousness but was patched up and stayed with his men. Here they stayed until relieved by 10/York and Lancs. He received the Military Cross in late August 1916 for his 'conspicuous gallantry' for organizing his men and leading them 'against the enemy'. Howe had originally wanted to join the Sheffield City Battalion. How might fate have treated him if he had succeeded and had gone over at Serre that morning?

The West Yorks lost 710 officers and men in the attack with at least another 150 dying of their wounds in the weeks that followed.

Many of the wounded would have been lying in no-man's-land and one such was 18-year-old **Private Thomas Almond** of 10/West Yorks, who took 2 hours to crawl 20yd with a broken leg before he was found and brought into the British lines. Others were not so lucky and died of wounds surrounded by the inert bodies of their dead comrades. Straddling the track ahead of you was 4/Middlesex and on its left – to the right of the track – was 8/Somerset Light Infantry under the command of **Lieutenant Colonel John Scott** and 9/ and 10/KOYLI of 64 Brigade who were west of the Willow Patch. **Lieutenant Bradford Gordon** witnessed the death of the 9/KOYLI commanding officer, Lieutenant Colonel Lynch, whose grave you visited in Norfolk Cemetery:

> The advance was by crawling and by rushes from shell hole to shell hole. The noise was deafening and the German machine-gun fire was terrible. Just before reaching the Russian Sap, I was struck on the chin by a piece of shrapnel. When I reached the Sap, I lay down and looked into it. I saw the CO, Colonel Lynch, who said, 'Hullo Gordon, are you hit?' The Colonel then began to get out of the Sap. He was killed by a shell almost immediately afterwards.

The battalion's advance south of the Willow Patch took the survivors across the Contalmaison road – referred to as the **Sunken Road** in numerous war diaries – to **Crucifix Trench** where they reorganized under the command of **Lieutenant Leonard Spicer**, who was one of a handful of officers still capable of offensive action. A later roll call revealed the battalion had suffered 490 casualties.

Now continue along the track in the direction of the single tree you will see ahead marking the junction ❼ of four tracks. This is the point at which our route touches the southeastern tip of **Route 8**, Bécourt is straight ahead and the Lochnagar mine crater is to the right. We are going to take the left-hand track which heads towards the Albert industrial complex you can see in the distance. Continue along the track and just after the track bends to the left stop ❽. The trees on the right – which were not there in 1916 – mask **Norfolk Cemetery** and the former site of **Queen's Redoubt** which sat on the 75m contour line above the cemetery and where Major Loudoun-Shand and 10/Yorkshire Regiment spent part of the night of 30 June 1916. Directly ahead is the bridge taking the D938 across the road that we travelled along during the la Boisselle to Fricourt Spine Route.

At the T-junction of tracks turn left ❾ and if the weather is clear you should be able to see the Cross of Sacrifice at Fricourt Military Cemetery (Bray Road) on your left. As you continue along the track the line of trees and shrubs on the right marks the pre-war railway line that ran between Fricourt and Bécourt and followed the line of the Vallée de Bécordel and the Vallée Reynard. In 1916 a light military railway also ran along the valley. Ignoring the first track on the right, continue for another 300m and stop. This is the point at which the British front line crossed the track in front of you from just west of Fricourt New Military Cemetery in the north, to Bois Français in the south. It was astride the track you are on that **Lieutenant Colonel Ronald d'Arcy Fife** and 7/Yorkshire Regiment began their 2.30pm assault on Fricourt. Although they were not part of the first wave, the day began badly when A Company under **Major Ralph Kent** had, for some inexplicable reason, begun their assault at 7.45am. Fife was speechless: 'I did not believe this but sent the Adjutant to find out. He reported that it was true. I could only account for this by supposing Kent had gone mad. Later a report came in saying that what was left of A Company were lying out in front of our wire, waiting for our artillery to lift.' Of the 140 men of A Company that attacked with Major Kent, 108 became casualties. Now devoid of one company, Colonel Fife, whose headquarters was in a dugout below the railway embankment near the former Fricourt station, awaited the orders that would send his battalion into action:

> A storm of fire met my men as they crossed the parapet and officers and men fell by scores. In about 1 minute all officers of B Company were hit, all of C Company except [Second Lieutenant Geoffrey Stapleton (Stapylton)] Roper so far as I have up to now ascertained and all of D Company except [company commander Captain Howard Leslie] Bartrum … I could see my men lying halfway between our trenches and the enemy's, most of them evidently dead or wounded. I came to the conclusion that any further advance would sacrifice my last remaining men.

Howard Bartrum's D Company lost sixty-one men that day. Bartrum went on to fight in other major campaigns and survived Passchendaele in 1917 only to die at the regimental depot in July 1918 aged 38 after the battalion had been disbanded. He is buried in Richmond Cemetery, North Yorkshire. Richmond-born Geoffrey Roper was another survivor of the carnage whose Military Cross – awarded for leading his platoon 'with great dash in the assault', afterwards crawling 'back to the trenches to make a report' before returning to his men 'under close and heavy fire the whole time' – was announced in the same issue of the *London Gazette* as that of Philip Howe. Roper had enlisted as a private in Princess Patricia's Canadian Light Infantry in August 1914 after emigrating to Canada. Commissioned into the Green Howards, he was killed on 12 May 1917 during the Battle of Arras and is buried in Cabaret Rouge British Cemetery, Souchez (XVII.AA.21)

Continue past the re-cycling plant – which is the approximate location of the former railway station – and the track becomes the Rue du 8 Mai 1945. At the junction with the D147 turn right and stop after 100m at **Fricourt British Cemetery (Bray Road)** ⑩.

The 7th Yorkshire Regiment Memorial at Fricourt British Cemetery.

The cemetery was begun by 7/Yorkshire Regiment's survivors and is in the former no-man's-land almost opposite the positions occupied by A Company, the northern wall of the cemetery lying alongside the German front line. There are eighty-nine casualties from this battalion buried here, fifty-nine of which are buried in communal graves in the centre of the cemetery. Further casualties were brought in later and there are now 133 burials here. The 7/Yorkshire Regiment originally erected a timber memorial in the cemetery listing 117 men killed in action which was replaced by the granite memorial you see in the right-hand corner. This may well be the only memorial of its kind erected within a CWGC cemetery. Of those commemorated on the memorial, 28-year-old **Second Lieutenant Harold Hornsby** (A.29) was on the solicitor's staff of his Majesty's Custom and Excise before he was commissioned in March 1915. He is remembered on the Saltburn War Memorial in Yorkshire. **Corporal William Vickers** (Sp Mem C.1) enlisted in Durham and is remembered on the Grangetown War Memorial. A former steel worker, he was one of seven children who lived at 48 Wren Street, Stockton-on-Tees. Killed in Fricourt Wood on 2 July during the capture of the village, 39-year-old **Major Robert Raper** (B.24A) of 8/South Staffordshires has the honour of a road in the village being named after him. His body was originally buried across the road from the cemetery and it was not until 1965 that the CWGC exhumed the body and buried it in its present position. The Rue Major Raper runs from the village war memorial to the church, the reconstruction of which was supported financially by the Raper family. Inside is a plaque dedicated to Major Raper and another commemorating the officers and men of the 17th Division who fell in France and Belgium.

The original 7/Yorkshires' Memorial was constructed in wood.

Leave the cemetery and continue uphill to the bend in the road, it was at this point that the former railway line crossed the road in front of you before following the valley round to Mametz. Continue to the crossroads and go straight across. Take care here as the road can be busy. Almost immediately on the right is **Fricourt Communal Cemetery** ⓫ where, towards the back of the plot, the crew of a 59 Squadron Bristol Blenheim was buried after being shot down nearby. After leaving the cemetery continue for another 300m to reach a track on the left ⓬ opposite a farm complex, and stop here for a moment. Behind the farm the track heading west towards Bécordel-Bécourt runs along the line of the former **Sandown Avenue Trench** to **Bonté Redoubt**. At the point where **Kingston Road Trench** meets **Sandown Avenue Trench** is the approximate position

Major Robert Raper.

of the vantage point on Crawley Ridge from where the poet **Lieutenant Siegfried Sassoon,** serving with C Company 1/Royal Welch Fusiliers – in support that day – had a clear view across the communal cemetery – as if from 'an opera box' according to his companion – to watch the 21st Division advance on 1 July. Sassoon ate an orange and saw a skylark as he observed 'a sunlit picture of hell' unfold below him.

Continue uphill along the track towards the Bois Français ⓭ which you can see ahead of you. About halfway up the track the British front line turned east to meander towards **Mansel Copse** and we pass into the 7th Division area and that of XV Corps. If you need to pause to catch your breath The Tambour mine craters can be seen behind you marked by the long line of trees and shrubs with the Willow Patch silhouetted on the skyline beyond. A few metres past the line of trees marking the edge of the **Bois Français** a narrow shingle pathway leads to the grave of a 34-year-old French soldier named **François Henri Thomassin**, who was killed in action on 30 September 1914 serving with the 26th Regiment of Infantry during the fighting for Fricourt during the war of manoeuvre on the Somme. Thomassin was killed near this spot but his original grave was lost and so, in his memory, the ground was purchased by the family post-war, although today it is well-maintained by *Souvenir Français*. Beyond this rather elaborate and isolated grave

The view across to the Willow Patch from the Bois Français.

The grave of François Thomassin, 26th Regiment of Infantry.

you can access part of the extensive British trench system of July 1916 still in existence in the woods.

After re-joining the track, continue uphill to the obvious crosstracks. Should you choose to visit the two Point 110 cemeteries, then turn right here following the CWGC signs. The track follows the approximate line of the former **Park Lane** communication trench and after 300m ⑭ you will come to **Point 110 Old Cemetery** on the right. The cemetery is situated on or close to the former site of **Maple Redoubt** which is mentioned on numerous occasions by Siegfried Sassoon and other writers. Begun by the French in February 1915, the cemetery drew its name from the height above sea level of the British positions south of the Bois Français and today contains 100 casualties of which 3 are unidentified. After September 1916 the area was known as King George's Hill. There are no 1 July casualties buried here but the first British soldier to be killed in this sector, **Private Frank Footman** (K.14) of 1/Duke of Cornwall's Light Infantry, who was killed on 2 August 1915, is buried in the right-hand corner. Continue to **Point 110 New Military Cemetery** which is 230m further along the track ⑮. The cemetery is the smaller of the two with sixty-four burials and contains

Point 110 Old Cemetery is on the right and Point 110 New Military Cemetery is 230m further along the track on the left.

two men who were killed on 1 July 1916. **Second Lieutenant C.S. Gibson** (D.10) and **Private Arthur Turner** (D.9) were both 23 years old and both serving with 22 Company of the Machine Gun Corps which was attached to the 7th Division.

Retrace your steps to the junction and stop. A windmill had, unsurprisingly given the lofty position, stood in the fields to the right where there are now the remnants of numerous mine craters, but a close examination of the rounded structures will reveal a concrete floor on which anti-aircraft guns were mounted during the Second World War, to protect the aeroplane factories – built by Henri Potez at Méaulte and Albert in the late 1920s – from German bombers. Opposite this field, at 2.30pm on 1 July, C Company of 20/Manchesters (5th City Battalion) was detailed to clear the craters and push on into **Bois Français Support Trench**. Within 10 minutes they had reached it but found themselves checked in **Zinc Trench** and **Orchard Alley**. Despite fierce fighting, they were forced back into the German second line where they consolidated.

The main Manchesters' attack was across the road – called the Sunken Road in many accounts – which heads north – down the slope and through Bois Français back towards Fricourt. This track, which passes the entrance to a *Ball Trap* – a clay pigeon shooting range – on the right, soon develops into a steep, metalled road which shadows the German front line – Aeroplane Trench – which ran along the crest of the slope in the fields to the right. Three companies of Manchesters went over the top from the fields to your left at 2.30pm and swept over the German front line to your right almost without casualties.

As you begin to head down the lane, imagine the Manchesters passing from left to right and be guided by the words of Siegfried Sassoon – who watched it all unfold from his vantage point some 650m away to your left and later wrote it up in his *Complete Memoirs of George Sherston*. Sassoon saw 'about 400' Manchesters who 'apparently took Sunken Road Trench', many walking 'casually across with sloped arms'. Here A and B companies swung too far to the right and came under a murderous fire from **Wing Corner** near the junction with the D938 at the bottom of the hill. Sassoon notes that they 'took about 40 casualties on the left' as machine-gun fire fell on them and these 'lay still in the sunlight whilst the swarm of figures disappeared over the hill'. ⓰ The commanding officer, **Lieutenant Colonel Harold Lewis**, was killed towards the bottom of the hill and two platoons of D Company were all but wiped out. Sassoon saw 'a cloud of pinkish smoke' hanging over Fricourt and after 20 minutes no-man's-land was empty 'except for the casualties about half way across'.

Continue downhill – Aeroplane Trench was in the fields to your right – to the junction at the bottom. Wing Corner was across to the left and it was here that A Company 1/RWF attacked alongside the Manchesters, silencing a particularly troublesome 'canister machine' – trench mortar – 'which for months had made itself a nuisance' and was 'claimed as a trophy the detachment being all killed by the [1/RWF] Bombers', according to the war diary.

Go straight across the main road with care and follow the road round to the left. You are now behind German lines and as the road swings round to the left you cross once more into the 21st Divisional area. Take the first turning on the right – Rue de la Place – to return to your vehicle.

Front Line Spine Route
Fricourt to Mametz

Distance: 2.4km/1.5 miles
Suitable for: 🚗 🚲

This is a very short section of road that runs between Fricourt and Mametz and was behind the German front line on 1 July 1916. From the war memorial at Fricourt the D464 – Rue du Marechal Foch – leads to the junction with the D64, and if traffic permits pause briefly here. The road layout is very similar to that of 1916, to your left a German light railway followed the line of **Willow Avenue** which ran along the southern side of the Vallée de Mametz, whilst across to your right is the **Bois Français** which we visited in **Route 9**. Continue into Mametz and park outside the church.

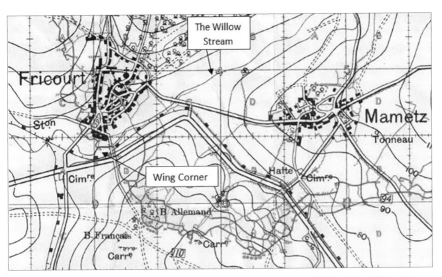

A section of trench map showing the German trenches around Fricourt and Mametz. The modern-day road system follows almost exactly the road layout that was in existence in 1916. Willow Stream, which acted as the divisional boundary between the 7th and 21st divisions, can be seen flowing in the valley between the two villages.

Route 10

Mametz

A circular tour beginning at: Mametz church
Coordinates: 49°59′48.98″ N – 2°44′05.44″ E
Distance: 4.0km/2.5 miles
Suitable for: ♦ ♿
Grade: Moderate (total ascent 66m)
Maps: IGN Série Bleue 2408E Bray sur Somme

General description and context: A short route that visits the communal cemetery and the Devonshire Cemetery and climbs the high ground south of Mansel Copse which on clear days provide panoramic views over the battlefield. The village of Mametz was held by RIR 23 and RIR 109 and captured by the 7th Division on 1 July. To the right of 20/Manchesters, who were in extended line opposite the Bois Français, was 20 Brigade consisting of 2/Border Regiment opposite **Danube Trench** and 9/Devons at **Mansel Copse** – so named on many trench maps of the time but marked as 'Mansell' on the British Official History maps – with 2/Gordon Highlanders on the north side of the D64 Péronne road. On the right was 91 Brigade with 1/South Staffs facing **Bulgar Point** and 22/Manchesters on the extreme right flank just south of **The Mound**. The five supporting battalions were in position behind the front line. Now ranged against the German line forming the horizontal bar of the letter 'L', these battalions would attack towards the north and northwest.

At 7.28am five small mines – four of 226kg (500lb) and one of 90kg (200lb) – were fired in the vicinity of **Kiel** and Danube Trenches 2 minutes before zero to destroy dugouts and machine-gun posts. They did the trick. After crossing **Danube Support Trench** 2/Border cleared **Hidden Wood** – south of the present-day D938 – and entered **Apple Alley** to secure its first objective. To the east the attack of 9/Devons resulted in huge casualties as the battalion was caught in the open by a machine gun positioned in the communal cemetery at **The Shrine**. Very few managed to cross no-man's-land to consolidate in **Tirpitz Trench**. 2/Gordon Highlanders were tasked with attacking towards **The Halt** – a small station on the Albert–Péronne railway – and the cemetery, but

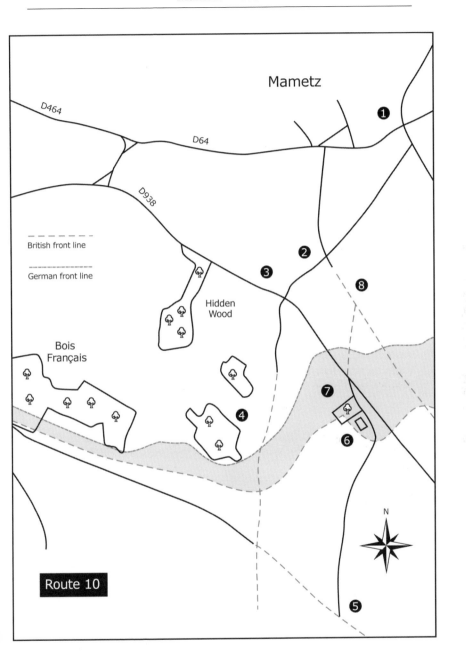

handicapped by the demise of the Devons on their left they pushed forward to reach **Shrine Alley** and, with support from 8/Devons, they took **Bunny Trench** north of Mametz by late afternoon.

The attack of 91 Brigade was heralded by the firing of three more small mines, which certainly helped 1/South Staffs, who were reported to be on the southern outskirts of Mametz at 7.45am, even though the large 907kg (2,000lb) charge under the **Bulgar Point Salient** failed to detonate. Quarter of an hour later 22/Manchesters occupied **Bucket Trench** and **Dantzig Alley** east of the village, assisted by 2/Queen's. But their advance had been costly and with 490 casualties amongst the officers and men the battalion had almost ceased to exist. Late that afternoon Mametz was placed under the command of **Lieutenant Colonel William Norman** of 21/Manchesters.

Directions to start: Mametz can be approached from the west by the D938 and from the east by the D64. The church is situated on the Rue de la Libération where there is parking. Alternatively, there is parking opposite the village war memorial.

Route description: Keeping the church on your left continue up the road to the village crossroads. On the left is the village war memorial together with the memorial to the 20th, 21st, 22nd and 24th battalions of the Manchester Regiment, which was erected by the Lancashire and

The memorial to the four Manchester battalions that took part in the assault on Mametz.

Cheshire Branch of the Western Front Association in October 2002. ❶
These battalions were amongst those which successfully captured the
village of Mametz on 1 July 1916.

Turn right at the crossroads – signposted Carnoy – along the Rue du
Moulin and bear right at the bend onto the Rue de l'Âtre to continue
downhill to the communal cemetery ❷ on the right. Stop here and
glance across to the right where the elongated **Hidden Wood** can be
seen on the hillside on the far side of the D938. From this point you
can also take in the uninterrupted view to the left across the D938 to
Mansel Copse where 9/Devons were positioned on 1 July. We shall
return to their story – and that of the communal cemetery – later.

Continue downhill along the line of the German **Shrine Alley
Trench** to the junction with the busy D938. Stop here. Across to your
right, now surrounded by trees and other vegetation, is the former
Mametz Halt railway station ❸ which was rebuilt after the war
and was on the ground north of the former railway line over which
2/Gordon Highlanders attacked. If you look left, the trees of Mansel
Copse mask the location of the Devonshire Cemetery.

*The disused former halt that served the Albert–Péronne railway was rebuilt after the
war.*

Directly opposite the junction is a metalled road heading uphill. Cross the busy carriageway with care here and take that road as it bends round to the left and ascends. After a short distance the metalled road becomes a track and 100m beyond that point the German front-line trenches cut across it to run diagonally back down the slope to your left in the direction of the main road and Mametz. The British front line lay another 180m further up the track. As you near the top of the rise the wooded copse across to the right ❹ is the site of the **Kiel Trench crater field** where Lieutenant Siegfried Sassoon's actions in bringing in the mortally wounded Corporal Richard 'Mick' O'Brien under fire during a raid on the night 25/26 May 1916 led to the award of his Military Cross, the ribbon of which, in 1917, he threw 'into the mouth of the Mersey' in a 'paroxysm of frustration' at the conduct of the war. He was unable to save O'Brien's life and the corporal – who had served on the Western Front since 6 October 1914 – is buried in the Citadel New Military Cemetery, 2.5km south of Fricourt (Grave III.F.17).

Apart from **Hidden Wood** (Blanc Fossé on IGN maps), which was cleared by C Company, 2/Border on 1 July 1916, the trench maps of the time only mark Bois Français and Mansel Copse; the two copses to the right of the track were planted with regular rows of trees after the war.

At the crossroad of tracks stop and turn towards Mametz to face the way you have come. You are now on the heights of the Montagne de Cappy, 112m above sea level. The track you have just climbed to reach this spot has come through the positions held by 2/Border Regiment on 1 July 1916. To their – and your – left, in front of the **Bois Français** which

The high ground south of the D938. The Bois Français can be seen on the skyline.

you can see clearly, were 20/Manchesters, whilst on the right were 9/Devons at Mansel Copse to the left of the two barns you can see. At 7.27am 2/Border advanced across Danube Trench towards Mametz in four lines passing Hidden Wood, which you noted earlier, before moving left to form a defensive flank east of Fricourt. **Lieutenant George Prynne** was in command of A Company and remembered forming up in the front-line trenches with C Company on his left and 9/Devons to his right:

> About 100 yards in the rear of [3 and 4 platoons] I came up with Nos. 1 and 2 platoons. The lines advanced in quick time, only losing at the most, two or three men before reaching the enemy's front line. This was crossed with comparative ease, and a few of the enemy showed themselves first in the support line. Some of these were killed or taken prisoner and a few fled down the communication trenches and disappeared.

The Border Regiment reported 243 officers and men as casualties after roll call on 3 July. This crossroads was also the location of **Wellington Redoubt**. At 7.30am 8/Devons moved up to this point before cutting across the fields towards Mansel Copse in support of 9/Devons.

Turn left here for 380m until you reach a T-junction. From this point – on a clear day – the village of Montauban will be visible on the skyline to the right and you may also be able to make out the Cross of Sacrifice at **Dantzig Alley Cemetery** to the left of Mansel Copse.

Turn left at the T-junction ❺ along the narrow metalled road which descends steeply towards Mansel Copse. As you draw closer to the D938 in the valley below, the track you are on swings round to the left and hits the British front line at the steps leading up to Devonshire Cemetery. The 9/Devons front-line trenches ran just inside the tree line of the copse. Stop here. Mansel Copse was named after **Second Lieutenant Spencer Lort Mansel Mansel-Carey** of 9/Devons who was mortally wounded here on 25 February 1916. His friend Captain Frank Wollocombe – who had been shot in the shoulder by a German sniper on 25 April 1916 leading a wiring party up near Wellington Redoubt where you were earlier – recorded in his diary that 'Mansel-Carey was killed by a rifle grenade today, I am sorry to say. He came out with me, was on the 7th Divisional course with me and we were at Wareham together.' Second Lieutenant Mansel-Carey is buried in Corbie Communal Cemetery (I.D.9).

Recalling the atmosphere at Mansel Copse, 19-year-old Private Albert Conn focused on a small but significant detail:

a little bird sings on a stunted tree in Mansell Copse [sic] at dawn. We used to listen to it. One morning that corporal of ours came round the corner and shot the poor bloody bird off the tree. A couple of the lads told him to f*** off out of it. Strange place this Mansell Copse … It's a bit lonely round that quarter. Always gives me the creeps when I have to go through there.

The story of the Devons at Mansel Copse is well documented and the tragic results of their advance can be found in the cemetery at the top of the steps. Before the battle **Captain Duncan Martin**, an artist by profession, had constructed a contoured model of the battlefield which, 20 Brigade HQ noted, showed 'the whole area to be attacked by the 20th Infantry Brigade also Fricourt Wood, Fricourt Farm, Railway Alley, Fritz Alley, Bright Alley'. The model – brought to France in a suitcase – was deemed so good that it found its way to Brigade HQ at Grovetown where all commanding officers were encouraged to send their officers to inspect it. Captain Martin prophesied that disaster would befall the battalion if the machine gun – located at the Shrine in Mametz Communal Cemetery and sited to pour enfilade fire into the right flank of the Devons – ❷ was not silenced before the battalion began its assault.

On 1 July 9/Devons left their assembly trenches and began their advance towards Danube Trench parallel to the line of the main road. The ground – creased by several shallow re-entrants at right angles to the assault – was clearly under the observation of the numerous machine-gun positions at Mametz – including the one at The Shrine. But they had not been silenced and Martin's tragic prediction came to pass. He and 455 officers and men were amongst the casualties. After the capture of Mametz, Captain Martin and 122 of the 9th Battalion and 38 of 8/Devons, who came up in support, were brought back to the front-line trench in Mansel Copse for burial on 3 July. The Revd Ernest Crosse, the Devons' chaplain, had taken a party of fifty men of 8/ and 9/ Devons to collect the dead.

'I met Riddell Webster who authorised me to bury in Mansell Copse. We made a collecting station at the foot of the copse where Sergt Newcombe collected identity discs and personal effects.' The following day Crosse recorded that 'All together we collected 163 Devons and covered them up in Mansell Copse. A colossal thunderstorm about 2.00pm delayed us sorely. At 6.00pm in the presence of the General [Deverell], Foss, Milne and about sixty men I read the funeral service and the "Thanksgiving for Victory". The working party was dead beat and the task of filling in the trench was awfully slow.' On 5 July Crosse 'got the Pioneer Sergt to paint a board with red lead borrowed from the RE's and then went up to Mansell Copse to mark the cemetery. I put up the board "Cemetery of 163 Devons – Killed July 1st 1916 – Devonshire 9". I planted twelve crosses in two rows, and after wiring in the area, I rode back to Ribemont [sur-Ancre] where the 9th had just arrived.'

Crosse's creation – **Devonshire Cemetery – ❻** now contains 163 casualties of which 10 are unidentified, and all but 2 – both Royal Artillery – are men of 8/ and 9/Devons. The present total of 161 possible Devons is therefore different to that stated by Ernest Crosse. At the top of the steps by the entrance is a poignant reminder that the 'The Devonshires held this trench and the Devonshires hold it still'. Originally inscribed on a wooden board it was replaced by the memorial stone you see now, unveiled by the Duke of Kent – Colonel in Chief of The Devonshire and Dorset Regiment and President of the CWGC – on 1 July 1986, the seventieth anniversary of the action. Looking over the far wall of the cemetery it is possible to see the continuation of the trench through the copse. Buried here is the war poet **Lieutenant Noel Hodgson** (A.3) who wrote 'Before Action' just days before his death. He was the fourth and youngest child of Henry Bernard Hodgson, the first Bishop of Saint Edmundsbury and Ipswich, and had been awarded the MC for actions at Loos in September 1915. Although he had been writing poetry since 1913, he started publishing stories and poems in periodicals at the beginning of 1916 under the name Edward Melbourne, his posthumous volume *Verse and Prose in Peace and War* was published in 1917 and ran to three editions. The son of the well-known Cornish painter Travers Patrick Adamson, 20-year-old **Second Lieutenant Travers Adamson** (A.7), died of his wounds. Another artist was 42-year-old **Second Lieutenant Percy Gethin** (B.4), an established painter, draughtsman and etcher who studied at the Westminster School of Art and at the *Atelier Colarossi* in Paris. Prior to his commission he taught life drawing at the Central School in London. At the far end of the cemetery 30-year-old **Captain Duncan Martin** (A.1)

'The Devonshires Held This Trench,
The Devonshires Hold It Still'.

Devonshire Cemetery.

from Brockenhurst, Hampshire shares a headstone with **Privates Frederick Oxford** and **Marshal Williams**. Close by is 31-year-old **Second Lieutenant Robert Davidson** (A.2), who was born in Singapore and attended Tunbridge School. Travelling to the then Ceylon, he took up a career as a planter before being commissioned in August 1915. He arrived in France three months before his death on 1 July and is also commemorated on the Ipoh War Memorial in Malaysia. London-born 19-year-old **Private Henry Inight** (A.7) enlisted in Exeter and lived with his widowed mother, Ada, and his younger brother, Edward, in Millman Street, Holborn. He was killed near **Swag Lane Trench** during the 8/Devons' advance.

Duncan Martin's plasticine model survived the war and went to the Royal United Services Institute (RUSI). The

Second Lieutenant Robert Davidson.

RUSI collections were subsequently acquired by the National Army Museum but there is now no record of its existence.

Leave the cemetery and turn left towards the main road. Should you wish to visit Gordon Cemetery, which is situated on the main road to your right, this is probably the most opportune moment but please take care crossing the road. **Gordon Cemetery** was begun by men of 2/Gordon Highlanders – the battalion attacked along the floor of the valley here – who buried some of their dead of 1 July, together with two artillerymen and an unknown soldier, in what had been a support trench. There are now 102 burials here of which 5 are unidentified. As the precise location of most of the graves could not be established, ninety-three of the headstones are arranged in semi-circles around the Cross of Sacrifice. To the right of the entrance are the graves of six second lieutenants (A.1–A.6) who are, unusually, buried together and separately from their men.

Our route from Devonshire Cemetery continues to bear left, passing Mansel Copse ❼ on the left to arrive at the D939. If you look left you should be able to see a track on the far side of the road some 50m further on. Cross the road with care and take this track and stop after 100m. You are now standing on the German front line, the line of the track roughly corresponding to the line of attack taken by the Devonshires as they left the British line in the direction of **Mametz Communal Cemetery**. The fields either side of the track would have been carpeted with the dead and dying of 20 Brigade cut down by the machine guns positioned in the

Gordon Cemetery.

The view from the communal cemetery across the D938 to Mansel Copse.

communal cemetery and on the high ground behind and to your left. At the junction of tracks ❽ bear left towards the communal cemetery, the entrance to which is 190m further along on the Rue St-Martin.

Walk to the far end of the cemetery until you have an uninterrupted view of Mansel Copse. This is the view the German machine-gunners had of the advancing British troops leaving their assembly trenches on the far side of the road. The obvious shrapnel marks on some of the cemetery memorials can be attributed to the Second World War when the area once again became a battlefield, although the damage appears to be of earlier vintage. From here you can see why the machine-gun post at The Shrine posed such a threat to the Devons as you look across the ground towards the Devonshire Cemetery. After leaving the cemetery turn right to reach the junction with Rue de la Libération where a right turn will take you back to your vehicle.

Front Line Spine Route
Mametz to Montauban

Distance: 3.4km/2.1 miles
Suitable for: 🚗 🚲

Before you drive towards Montauban you may wish to deviate slightly to the point where the 22/Manchesters advanced from the British front line at **The Mound** on the extreme right flank of the 7th Division area. To reach The Mound turn right at the village crossroads opposite the war memorial and continue towards Carnoy for 700m where a large barn and track on the left mark the approximate position of the German front line. Approximately 150m further along the road rises over The Mound, which is where the British front line crossed the road with 22/Manchesters straddling the road facing towards Mametz. **Bulgar Point**, beneath which was the large mine that failed to detonate on 1 July due to severed leads, was about 300m west of The Mound with **Austrian Trench** to the east. It was whilst the Manchesters were waiting here for zero on 1 July that 27-year-old **Captain Charlie May** completed his last letter to his wife, Bessie:

> 5.45am. It is a glorious morning and is now broad daylight. We go over in two hours' time. It seems a long time to wait and I think whatever happens, we shall all feel relieved once the line is launched. No man's land is a tangled desert. Unless one could see it one cannot imagine what a terrible state of disorder it is in.

Retrace your steps to the village crossroads and turn right to follow CWGC signposts for **Dantzig Alley British Cemetery** which you will find 500m further along the road on the left. The boundary between the 7th and **Major General Ivor Maxse's** 18th Division crossed the road 150m further still. This is a large concentration cemetery containing 2,053 casualties of which 518 are unidentified which means men from several burial grounds in the area have been re-interred here. Two of these are 30-year-old **Lieutenant Harold Hillman** (VI.A.3), who was killed with 7/Green Howards on 1 July at Fricourt, and 28-year-old **Corporal William Brown** (VI.T.3), who was killed with 10/West

Yorkshires at Fricourt on 1 July after enlisting at Leeds (see **Route 9**). The former printer's compositor was married to Elizabeth and boarded with the Matthews family at Cankerwell Lane.

The cemetery stands close to where 22/Manchesters and 2/Queen's took **Dantzig Alley Trench** which was just south of the D64. The view from the rear wall of the cemetery is remarkably fine and on a clear day it is possible to see **Mametz Wood** and the Longueval Ridge which were to figure so much in the coming months of the Somme campaign, whilst in the foreground, marked by the line of trees and shrubs, is **Queen's Nullah** where **Major General Edward Ingouville-Williams** became the most senior of the Somme casualties when he was killed by a shell at 7.00pm on 22 July 1916. Two memorials are set into the wall of the cemetery, the first of which – commemorating the men of the Royal Welch Fusiliers – is on the left just inside the entrance. At the back of the cemetery is the 14/Royal Welch Fusiliers Memorial seat overlooking **Mametz Wood** where they lost so heavily on 10 July.

The CWGC database records 712 identified casualties of 1 July 1916, one of which is **Captain Charlie May** (II.B.3) of the 22/Manchesters who wrote such descriptive letters to his wife, Bessie, and hoped he 'may do his duty'. Serving in the same battalion was **Captain Alfred Bland** (IX.B.6), who enclosed a pressed flower – a forget-me-not – with his last message to his wife. An articled clerk to his father's firm of solicitors in Southport, 23-year-old **Second Lieutenant Frank Brooks** (V.I.9) was killed fighting with 20/Manchesters, as was 39-year-old **Captain Douglas Wilberforce** (VI.I.3), the medical officer attached to 20/Manchesters and who probably knew Frank Brooks. Both men were killed on 1 July near the Bois Français. Graduating in 1901, Wilberforce was assistant house-surgeon to Guy's Hospital and later Emden

The memorial plaque to the Royal Welch Fusiliers.

On the rear wall of the cemetery, overlooking Mametz Wood, is the memorial bench to 14th Royal Welch Fusiliers.

Scholar in the cancer research laboratory of the Middlesex Hospital. Nearby is the grave of 35-year-old **Lieutenant Colonel Harold Lewis** (VI.I.1), who commanded 20/Manchesters on 1 July. Buried only yards from where he was killed in **Beetle Alley Trench** is 31-year-old **Second Lieutenant William Savage** (II.D.1) of 11/Royal Fusiliers, 18th Division, who was instrumental in capturing the Pommiers Redoubt. **Captain Charles Brockbank** (V.U.8) was 32 years old when he was killed on 1 July leading 1 Company of 18/King's (Liverpool) Regiment. Shot twice by a machine gun near **Brick Lane Trench**, he refused to seek shelter and continued to cheer his men on, shouting 'go on number one'. His headstone bears the epitaph: 'That Life is Long That Answers Life's Great End – Duty and Love Rest in God'.

Captain Charlie May.

Leave the cemetery and continue along the D64 in the direction of Montauban, the church spire of which will soon come into view ahead, and 800m after leaving the cemetery you will see a track on the right. A few metres beyond this was the site of the German strongpoint called the **Pommiers Redoubt** – known by the Germans as *Jamin Werk* – which dominated the crest of the low spur you are ascending. On 1 July 1916 11/Royal Fusiliers were held up in **Pommiers Trench** – 370m or so south of the D64 – until 8.00am when the British artillery barrage assisted their advance to Pommiers Redoubt. Although faced with belts of barbed wire which were hidden from observation by the long grass and vegetation, the Fusiliers managed to outflank the redoubt's garrison, allowing **Second Lieutenant Savage** and his men to rush

Captain Charles Brockbank.

Beetle Alley Trench and break into the redoubt, which was in British hands by 9.30am. Compared with many units that attacked that day, the battalion's losses of 222 officers and men were comparatively light.

Just before you enter Montauban you will see a grey stone cross on the left of the road opposite the site of the former village windmill. Take care here as parking is difficult and the monument is easy to miss. Marked on IGN maps as a *tombe*, the memorial commemorates **Captaine Henri Thiérion de Monclin** of the 69th Regiment of Infantry who was killed during the German advance on 28 September 1914. Already carrying an old wound, de Monclin refused to leave the battlefield when the Germans attacked and he was hit again. Sharing bars of chocolate with his men, he remarked, 'It's over – we won't need any provisions'. The Germans came on in numbers and he was hit once more and killed along with half his company whilst covering the withdrawal of another battalion. Born in Paris in 1883, de Monclin had been a cadet at the military college at Saint-Cyr and was a *Chevalier de la Légion d'Honneur* and holder of the *Médaille Militaire*, *Croix de Guerre* and *Médaille du Maroc*. He is also remembered on a private calvary erected in 1926 by Charles de Granut Bigault in the commune of Vienne le Château in the Argonne. As there are no official burial records it is possible that the remains of de Monclin were recovered and are buried under the monument given that it is marked as a *tombe* rather than a monument. **High Wood** can be seen in the distance behind the memorial.

It is believed that Capitaine *Henri Thiérion de Monclin is buried near this spot.*

Continue into the village passing the church of St Giles on the left to take the next right turning – Rue de la Place – where your vehicle can be parked in the shade of the trees surrounding the village green.

Route 11

Montauban

A circular tour beginning at: **Montauban**
Coordinates: **50°00′22.41″ N – 2°46′52.66″ E**
Distance: **7.9km/4.9 miles**
Suitable for: 🚶 🚲
Grade: **Moderate (total ascent 87m)**
Maps: **IGN Série Bleue 2408E Bray sur Somme**

General description and context: The XIII Corps attack was divided into three phases, the first of which – the capture of Montauban – was detailed for 1 July 1916. On the right flank, with the village as its objective, was the 30th Division (**Major General John 'Jimmy' Shea**), its boundary with Maxse's 18th Division running along the western edge of the wooded la Longue Haie (Talus Boisé on British trench maps) and following the road running north, up to the junction of roads at the western extremity of the village. The 18th Division was tasked with the capture of Montauban Alley and Pommiers Redoubt before pushing on towards Caterpillar Wood.

The right flank of the 30th Division assault involved 17/ and 20/King's (Liverpool) Regiment and was remarkably successful. **Lieutenant Colonel Bryan Fairfax,** commanding 17/King's, stepped over the parapet with **Commandant Le Petit**, commanding the 3rd Battalion of the 153rd Regiment of Infantry, and both arrived in **Dublin Trench** – their first objective – together at 8.30am. A group of the enemy in **German's Wood** (today's la Garenne du Petit Charme) was taken prisoner on the way and the troops were delighted to find Dublin Trench unoccupied. On the King's left flank 21 Brigade achieved similar success, crossing the German line with very few casualties with the leading battalions – 19/Manchesters and 18/King's, along with 2/Yorkshire Regiment (Green Howards) and 2/Wiltshires in support – moving quickly along Railway Valley until they were held up by the British artillery barrage at **Alt Trench**. Moving closely behind the barrage, 18/King's came under machine-gun fire in the vicinity of **Train Alley Trench** from a German strongpoint called **The Warren** in the 18th Divisional area. Most of the 500 casualties

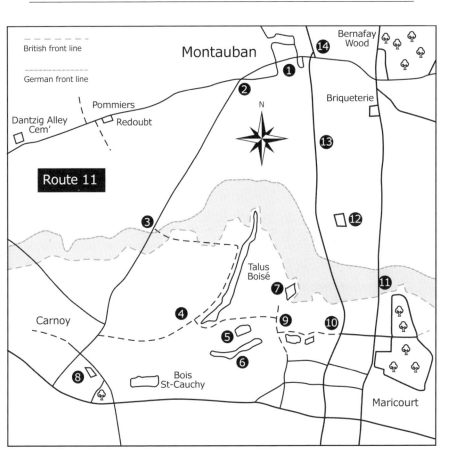

sustained by 18/King's on 1 July occurred here. Behind them, 2/Green Howards were hit hard in no-man's-land suffering over 200 casualties. At 8.30am, 21 Brigade finally reached the **Glatz Redoubt** to consolidate the line with 89 Brigade.

Just east of Talus Boisé, 90 Brigade was given the task of capturing Montauban with 16/ and 17/Manchesters leading the assault and 18/Manchesters and 2/Royal Scots Fusiliers in support. However, if the brigade was to have any chance of success then the **Glatz Redoubt** would have to be captured by 21 Brigade. At 8.30am the Manchester battalions began their advance after signal flares from the redoubt and a smoke screen courtesy of 4/Mortar Company indicated that the advance on the right had been successful. Held up temporarily by machine-gun fire from **The Warren**, the Manchesters – strengthened by 2/Royal Scots

Fusiliers – surged forward through Glatz Redoubt and over **Southern Trench** taking the village.

In the 18th Divisional area a large mine was detonated under the enemy salient at **Casino Point** at 7.27am. Taking advantage of the confusion, the leading battalions of 54 Brigade on the left flank – 11/Royal Fusiliers and 7/Bedfords – crossed the German front line without serious opposition until the Bedfords were held up by a machine gun firing from **The Triangle**. Many of their 321 casualties were sustained here and with practically every officer killed or wounded the attack was carried forward by the remaining NCOs and men. The attack by the 11/Fusiliers we have already looked at (see the Front Line Spine Route – Mametz to Montauban). Suffice it to say, the Fusiliers and 7/Bedfords were part of one of the most successful advances of the day.

The 53 Brigade attack was in the centre of the 18th Divisional assault with the 10/Essex in support and the 6/Royal Berks and the 8/Norfolks leading the attack. The Berks were opposite **Casino Point** which the Germans had strengthened with additional fire power, unaware that 183/Tunnelling company had laid 2,267kg (5000lb) of ammonal under the position. In their eagerness to get across no-man's-land the Royal Berks began their advance before the mine was detonated. **Lance Corporal Fisher** of 10/Essex was about 100yd from the explosion which rose in front of him in a great column of earth and chalk. He watched with amazement as large slabs of earth landed on some of the advancing troops forcing the battalion adjutant, **Lieutenant Randolph Chell,** to take cover. Chell wrote that the debris 'filled the air around us with lumps of chalk of varying sizes and a fair number of our men were injured by them'. Apart from suffering a few casualties from falling debris, the Royal Berks crossed the German front line and reached the eastern end of Pommiers Trench at 7.50am. Held up by the slower advance of 8/Norfolks, it was not until Pommiers Redoubt had been taken that the 54 Brigade battalions were able to move on towards **Montauban Alley Trench** – the German *Staubwasser Graben*.

The attack by 55 Brigade west of the Talus Boisé consisted of 8/East Surreys with 7/Queen's (Royal West Surrey) Regiment on their left with 7/Royal East Kent Regiment (The Buffs) in support and 7/Royal West Kents in reserve. This sector contained the **Carnoy craters**, just east of the Montauban–Carnoy road, which had been strengthened by the Germans. Their capture was the responsibility of B and half of D companies 7/Buffs. When the attack was launched fierce machine-gun fire from the Carnoy craters and **Breslau Trench** held up the whole advance until 7/Buffs were able to clear the crater field so ensuring the advance could continue. Although held up several times by machine-gun fire, the capture of Pommiers Redoubt relieved the pressure on 55 Brigade and as the German defenders began to fall back the present-day D64 Mametz–Montauban road was reached at around 3.00pm. Here a Queen's storming party led by **Second Lieutenant Herbert Tortise** overwhelmed a machine-gun post at **Blind Alley Trench** on the western edge of Montauban, capturing the trench and twelve of the enemy and then went on to overpower another post containing three machine guns: 'For three hours it held out. Lieutenant Tortise who had the Maxse dictum –"Kill Germans"– ingrained in him, made a dash at them. He and his dozen men got right amongst the enemy, bayoneted several of them and ended in possession of the post.'

Directions to start: Montauban is on the D64 which runs from Mametz to Montauban and on to Guillemont. There is ample parking around the village green east of the church on the opposite side of the road.

Route description: From your vehicle ❶ take the Rue de la Place back to the main road and turn left. Continue for 200m to the *Mairie* where you will find the village war memorial on the right and a small plaque celebrating the links between Montauban and Maidstone in the porch. Now take the Rue Neuve which is directly opposite the *Mairie* and will lead you past private houses to a junction ❷ with the D64. The narrow road on the left just before the junction marked the divisional boundary between the 18th Division – to the west – and the 30th – to the east. Ignore this road – it leads to Talus Boisé but turns into a track halfway down – and take the road on the left after another 25m – signposted Carnoy – which heads downhill and provides good views of the Basilique Notre Dame de Brebières at Albert and the square buildings of the airfield southeast of Méaulte across to the right. On 1 July 1916 this road was well behind German lines and we are now heading southwest – along the line of **Mine Alley** – across the Plaine de Carnoy towards the German front and support lines.

After 1.5km or so from the road junction at Montauban you will see a track on the left heading towards a line of trees in the distance. ❸ The track is metalled for the first 150m and easy to miss,

The Montauban village war memorial.

particularly if you are using bikes. Stop here. You are now in what was no-man's-land, but just 50m to your left, as you look east along the track towards the wooded expanse of the Talus Boisé, the **Carnoy Crater Field** began and ran away diagonally across the field to the northeast. Here the British and German lines were separated only by the width of numerous mine craters – at least ten, many of which overlapped. The British pushed out saps across the track in front of you from their front line to secure the southerly lips of the craters. The Germans held the northerly rims. This area was eventually captured by **Second Lieutenant Valentine Tatam** and B Company of the 7/Buffs. The war diary tells us it took 6 hours to clear the craters, which is why the 55 Brigade advance was held up for so long. Although the craters have been filled in, one can clearly pick out the darker circles of vegetation which mark the craters due to the disturbed soil below when the crops have been harvested in summer, and the IGN map marks several depressions in the ground at this point – look closely and you will notice them.

Turn right to look down the road towards Carnoy. The British front line ran parallel to the road to the left and crossed it some 200m further on, 8/Norfolks straddled the road there prior to going 'over the top'. Now turn right again to look west into the fields. The small German salient at **Casino Point** was situated 400m along the German front line – **Mine Trench** – almost exactly due east. It was the explosion at Casino Point – 20 seconds too late – that prompted **Lieutenant Randolph Chell** of the Royal Berks to take cover from the debris that seemed to fill the air. The vestiges of the crater were still there in the early 1980s but it has

The view from the Carnoy road looking east towards the Talus Boisé.

now gone. It was also in the fields in front of you that British tunnellers dug numerous saps to blow smaller dugout-destroying mines and to edge machine-gun and trench-mortar teams closer to the German lines at zero. Also employed, just metres away from you, were two huge Livens flame projectors – each weighing 2 tons – in saps just 54m from Mine Trench. Imagine now these behemoths roaring into life at 7.27am as they spewed their liquid fire into the German trenches opposite. See the billowing black smoke, feel the heat and smell the acrid fumes as you think of the forty or so German infantry who were incinerated alive whilst others escaped with singed hair and burnt bodies.

Turn 180° and continue along the track towards the woodland – Talus Boisé – which you can see in the distance. You will pass the site of a large crater after 100m to the right of the track. The German front line at this point – **Breslau Trench** – was in the fields to the left of the track and ran east to **Breslau Point**, before looping north and crossing the neck of the cleft – **Valley Trench** – which carried the Albert–Péronne light railway, north of Talus Boisé. The British front line followed a more meandering course along the track and enveloped the northern end of Talus Boisé before sweeping southeast towards Machine Gun Wood. If you turn towards Montauban and look uphill you will have the same view the attacking battalions of 55 Brigade had on 1 July as they began their assault on the village. Having passed along the front line where 7/Queen's were awaiting zero, the track descends gently downhill, and across to your left the British front line jutted forward in the form of a salient. It was here – in the slight hollow between higher ground either side, 200m away in the fields to the north – as 8/East Surreys were preparing to begin their assault, that one of the most famous and enduring events of the 'first day' of the Battle of the Somme took place. **Captain Wilfred 'Billie' Nevill**, commanding B Company, had been to see Captain Alfred Irwin a few days prior to 1 July with a strange request:

[Nevill] thought it might be helpful, as he had 400 yards to go and knew that it would be covered by machine-gun fire … if he could furnish each platoon with a football and allow them to kick it forward and follow it … and I sanctioned that on condition that he and his officers really kept command of their units and didn't allow it to develop into a rush after the ball. If a man came across a football he could kick it forward but he mustn't chase after it, and I think myself it did help them enormously, took their minds off it. But they suffered terribly. Nevill and his second captain were both killed.

With one ball said to be bearing the slogan 'The Great European Cup-Tie Final – East Surreys v Bavarians. Kick off at zero' and another 'NO REFEREE', Neville is said to have 'kicked off' one of the footballs with his second-in-command, **Lieutenant Robert 'Bobbie' Soames**, booting a second into no-man's-land. All went well until the British barrage lifted and then B Company were hit by heavy enfilade fire from the left flank from the area of the crater field you have just come from and Breslau Point. Their progress was watched by **Private Robert Cude**, a battalion runner with 7/Buffs:

One of the two footballs used in the 8th East Surreys' assault. This one is kept in the Queen's Regimental Museum.

> Soon after the lads get going, we can see that contrary to expectation we are not to have things all our own way. Here I may add that I am up forward with a message and determine to stop and see a bit of the fun. Jerry's machine guns open a terrific fire on our chaps and the first wave is speedily decimated. Others jump forward and fill the gaps. I am aghast at the accuracy of the fire. He has plenty of machine guns and is making a frightful carnage.

Captain Alfred Irwin, who survived the East Surreys' attack, was left almost shell shocked. 'All my best chaps had gone. We buried eight young officers in one grave before we left. It was a terrible massacre …We'd come down from 800 men to something under 200 in that attack, and it seemed to me a dreadful waste of life.' Irwin's estimation of the losses was fairly accurate: the battalion's casualties numbered 538 officers and men, some of which – including Billie Nevill – are buried in **Carnoy Military Cemetery** and can be visited at the conclusion of the Spine Route from Montauban to Maricourt. Two footballs were recovered: one is now held at Dover Castle – Captain Nevill was Head Boy of Dover College – and the other is in the regimental museum at Guildford. Interestingly, the war diary talks of 'four footballs', as does Captain Irwin, although many sources, including the Nevill family and Lieutenant Charles Alcock, a Surreys officer, cite two.

Continue downhill to the northwestern edge of the Talus Boisé, which was in the area of the 21 Brigade assault. Here it is possible to follow the edge of the wood to its northern tip. Looking north from here you can see how the attacking battalions were actually hidden from German view until they crested the hill ahead. Once they were sky-lined machine guns would have opened fire on them from Breslau Point.

Retrace your steps and continue along the western edge of the wood. Concealed from German observation the wood hosted the British reserve positions, communication trenches and dugouts – the remnants of which can still be seen today. In 1916 the wood would have contained numerous trench-mortar positions and the Albert–Péronne light railway ran along this same track towards Carnoy, along which many of the wounded from the 1 July assault were evacuated.

Captain Alfred Irwin survived the war and died in 1976.

At the southern end of the wood keep a sharp look out for an indistinct grass track on the left ❹ – very easy to miss – which will take you uphill to **Cambridge Copse** – marked on IGN maps as la Garenne Gustin – on the right ❺ and the elongated **Oxford Copse** ❻ behind. This is the area where 90 Brigade assembled in the early hours of 1 July prior to their attack on Montauban. Imagine now hundreds of men stirring here in the early dawn of 1 July as the light grew stronger revealing the long lines of khaki-clad men all around, their faces stern and gripping their rifles. Imagine too the bark of a long line of field guns – wheel-to-wheel just down the slope as they opened fire as one in the final bombardment. **Private Edward Jarman Higson** of 16/Manchesters remembered waiting for the order to move in the third wave:

> over went the first wave of men, the Liverpool Pals. They reached their objective, the German second line, with very few casualties … It was our job to capture the village of Montauban and at 7.25am we got out of our trench and … off we started, just as if we were doing a drill exhibition in England … We scrambled over our old trenches, reached the German second, then the third line, wounded men of the other two waves shouting out to us 'Good luck Manchesters'.

Suddenly the Manchesters were caught by German shells and their ranks were swept with machine-gun fire from the left. Higson continues: 'Our fellows were falling right and left, the noise of our guns and the firing of the enemy's made it impossible to hear orders.' Edward Higson fought through and after several close shaves he and the surviving 16/Manchesters finally reached their objective – Montauban Alley, some 350m north of where you parked your vehicle – by 10.30am. Here he met strong opposition, one team of machine gunners firing point blank at us until we overpowered them', but German resistance was finally crushed. He had been in action for 3 hours – much of that being hard fighting – and had covered a distance of 2.5km!

The following day 16/Manchesters were relieved and Edward Higson trudged back the 2.5km to this spot again, 'over the battle field of yesterday, now strewn with thousands of our boys and the enemy. It was awful to see the boys who 48 hours ago were full of life, now lying upon the battle field.' They picked up as many wounded as they could and delivered them to dressing stations before arriving back here to answer the roll. 'The Sergeant Major was there calling out the names – some were answered, others would never hear their names again on this earth but by this time would be answering the roll on the other side.'

The 2/Wiltshires and 2/Green Howards were also assembled along this track before moving up in support of the 21 Brigade attack. Continue to the junction of tracks ahead and stop. To your left ❼ is **Machine Gun Wood** – la Garenne Simon – and on the skyline, to the left – north – of Maricourt, are the two flagpoles marking the spot where the French and British front lines joined. If you turn round you will be able to see ❽ Carnoy Military Cemetery.

Bear right at the junction of tracks and, keeping the small copse on the left ❾, take the next grass track on the left which you will see immediately before another small copse. Take this track as it rises gently to follow the perimeter of the woods before it bends right to reach ❿ a road. Turn left here towards Montauban along the single-track metalled road. Continue along the road for approximately 250m and stop. On your left you should be able to see Machine Gun Wood, an integral part of the British front line, which ran across the road where you are standing towards **Maricourt Wood** and the two flagpoles ⓫ on your right. We will visit this site on the final leg of our journey along the spine of the front line. You are now in the 89 Brigade sector of the attack and the spot where you are standing is where the officers and men of 17/King's formed up prior to the attack. Behind them were 2/Bedfords

German's Wood can be seen on the right with the village of Montauban on the skyline.

on the northern outskirts of Maricourt before they moved across the road through German's Wood to **Dublin Trench**.

In another 450m you will cross the German front line which was known as **Silesia Trench**. Just after you pass German's Wood (la Garenne du Petit Charme) ⑫ the road begins to climb gently and as you reach the top of the rise stop again. This is the site of the German stronghold of the **Glatz Redoubt** ⑬ which straddled the road here and was taken at approximately 8.35am by 19/Manchesters, led by **Lieutenant James Higgins** and the men of 11 Platoon.

The road now rises steeply into Montauban to meet the main road. A track comes in from the left a little further on which approximates

The view that Lieutenant James Higgins and 11 Platoon of the 19th Manchesters would have had after capturing the Glatz Redoubt.

the course of **Train Alley** and 150m beyond that you will be able to trace a raised bank of scrub which marks the line of the same light railway you followed earlier. It ran from here down to Talus Boisé and on to Carnoy. Continue to the junction. You will find the Manchester and Liverpool Pals Memorial ⑭ on the right. Designed by Peter Sheard, the memorial was unveiled by Major General Peter Davies, Colonel of the King's Regiment, on 1 July 1994. On one face it carries the regimental badge – the eagle and child – of the Liverpool Service Battalions and on the other the regimental badge of the Manchester battalions that captured the village on 1 July 1916. The British line was consolidated on 1 July just north of the

The Liverpool and Manchester Pals Memorial at Montauban.

village, a point you can reach by continuing along the road opposite the memorial – signposted Quarry Cemetery – for approximately 250m to a farm track on the right. Continue past this junction for a few more metres and then look back towards the village. The tree line and the hedge marks the approximate line of **Montauban Alley Trench**. Retrace your steps to the Pals Memorial and turn right to return to your vehicle.

Montauban to the Maricourt Anglo/French Junction

Distance: 3.2km/1.9 miles
Suitable for: 🚗 🚲

This is the final stage of the journey (see **Route 11** map) along the front line of 1 July 1916. From Montauban pass the Pals Memorial and head east along the D64 towards the crossroads at the southeastern corner of **Bernafay Wood**. Turn right here along the D197 – passing the narrow road to Guillemont on your left – to reach the site of the **Briqueterie** on the right of the road after 250m. This area is now private property but was subjected to an artillery barrage at 11.30am by the divisional artillery, after which it was captured by **Captain Ernest Orford** and 4 Company of 20/King's. They reported the position here – and in the triangle of trenches created by Briqueterie Trench and Chimney Trench which followed the 'sunken' road to Guillemont in the fields opposite – under British control by 12.45pm. Parking here is difficult and there is very little left for the battlefield tourist to see. Orford was killed on 30 July 1916.

As you continue down the road look across to the right to the ground over which the 30th Division attacked northwards to Montauban. After another 1.6km you will come to the Anglo/French junction where the two front lines met on 1 July, marked by two flagpoles flying the French and British national flags. An information board shows a trench map of the area marking the two fronts. Little is known of **Commandant Le Petit,** commanding 3rd Battalion of the 153rd Regiment of Infantry. He was wounded in August 1916 and apparently left the battalion a short time later. However, **Lieutenant Colonel Bryan Fairfax**, commanding 17/King's, had already served in China and South Africa before he was recalled from the reserve in 1914 and appointed to command one of the Liverpool Pals battalions. He was gassed near Trones Wood on 29 July 1916 and after recovering in England he returned to France a year later to command the Chinese Labour Corps Headquarters.

The point where the British and French lines met is marked today by the national flags of the two nations.

Our tour of the 1 July front line terminates here but to conclude you may wish to visit Carnoy Military Cemetery, which is a short distance away.

From the Anglo/French flagpoles continue south along the D197 through Maricourt to the junction with the D938. Turn right and follow the road for approximately 2km until directed by CWGC signposts to Carnoy Military Cemetery.

Carnoy Military Cemetery

The cemetery originally stood just south of the site of the small railway 'halt' on the light railway which brushed the western edge of Talus Boisé and ran south of Montauban northeast, through Bernafay and Trones Woods on its way to Péronne. Begun in August 1915 by 2/KOSB and 2/KOYLI, the number of burials was considerably increased after the fighting of 1 July 1916. Today the cemetery contains 837 casualties, 29 are unidentified. Of this number fifty-seven men are casualties of 1 July and are largely from the XIII Corps brigades which attacked Montauban, whilst at least another fifteen men died on subsequent days of wounds received on 1 July. The cemetery is probably best known as the last resting place of **Captain Wilfred 'Billie' Nevill** (E.28), who commanded B Company of 8/East Surreys. One of nine children, he was educated at Dover College and Jesus College, Cambridge before being commissioned into the East Yorkshire Regiment. After attending Staff College he was attached to 8/East Surreys, a battalion he arrived in France with in 1915. He was one of the eight officer casualties sustained by the battalion on 1 July, six of whom share just

Captain William 'Billie' Nevill.

three headstones, whilst Nevill appears to be the only officer with his own headstone which displays the badge of the East Yorkshires, not his beloved 8/East Surreys. Nevill's second-in-command, 21-year-old **Lieutenant Robert Soames** (E.30), was at Oriel College, Oxford when he enlisted in the Public Schools Brigade in August 1914. Commissioned in September of that year, he was wounded a year later, returning to France in February 1916. He is buried next to 22-year-old **Captain Charles Pearce** (E.30), who commanded 8/East Surreys C Company, a man whom Nevill described as 'rather quaint but tolerable'. Like so many of the men who volunteered in 1914, Pearce was destined

Lieutenant Robert Soames.

Captain Charles Pearce.

for an altogether different career after leaving Winchester and Christchurch College, Oxford, but, like Nevill, was cut down in the fields north of Talus Boisé. **Captain Bernard Ayre** (D.10) of 8/Norfolks was the brother of Captain Eric Ayre of the Newfoundland Regiment (see Front Line Spine Route, Beaumont Hamel to Ulster Tower) who is buried at Ancre British Cemetery. Bernard Ayre was 24 years old when he was killed leaving **Bund Support Trench** – halfway between the German front line and the Mametz–Montauban road – just after 8.00am. **Second Lieutenant Frank Rushton** (Q.25) of 53 Trench Mortar Battery, 18th Division, was 30 years old when he was killed by a sniper in **Montauban Alley Trench** on 1 July. A former press correspondent at the *Daily Despatch*, he hailed from Darwin in Lancashire.

Appendix I

Where to Find the VC Winners

Although fifty-one Victoria Crosses were awarded over the course of the Battle of the Somme between 1 July and 18 November 1916, eight VCs were won by serving soldiers on the opening day of the battle. Six of those men are buried in cemeteries or commemorated on memorials within the area covered by this guidebook and were either killed during the action that resulted in their award or died soon afterwards from wounds received.

Name	Burial/Commemoration	Reference
Bell, Captain Norman Frankland *9/Royal Inniskilling Fusiliers*	Thiepval Memorial	
Green, Captain John Leslie *RAMC*	Foncquevillers Mil Cemetery	III.D.15
Loudoun-Shand, Major Stewart *10/Yorkshire Regiment*	Norfolk Cemetery	I.C.77
McFadzean, Private William *14/Royal Irish Rifles*	Thiepval Memorial	
Turnbull, Sergeant James *17/Highland Light Infantry*	Lonsdale Cemetery	IV.G.9
Cather, Lieutenant Geoffrey *9/Royal Irish Fusiliers*	Thiepval Memorial	

Appendix 2

Where to Find the Soldier Poets

The 'soldier poets' were a group of individuals who expressed their responses to the experience of war through their poetry. Some were already established writers and poets but others were not, finding their literary work inspired by the war in which they found themselves. Twelve of these soldier poets were killed on the Somme during 1916, six on the opening day of the battle. Many of these poets are largely unsung today and are only remembered on the headstones and memorials that are scattered across the battlefield.

Name	Date of Death	Burial/Commemoration
Freston, 2/Lieutenant Rex *6/Royal Berkshire Regiment*	Jan 1916	Bécourt Mil Cemetery I.E.16
Streets, Sergeant John *12/York and Lancaster Regiment*	July 1916	Euston Road Cemetery A.6
Ratcliffe, Lieutenant Alfred *10/West Yorkshire Regiment*	July 1916	Fricourt New Mil Cemetery C.8
Robertson, Corporal Alexander *12/York and Lancaster Regiment*	July 1916	Thiepval Memorial
Hodgson, Lieutenant William *9/Devonshire Regiment*	July 1916	Devonshire Cemetery A.3
Waterhouse, 2/Lieutenant Gilbert *2/Essex Regiment*	July 1916	Serre Road Cemetery No. 2 I.K.23

Name	Date of Death	Burial/Commemoration
White, Lieutenant Bernard *20/Tyneside Scottish*	July 1916	Thiepval Memorial
Winterbotham, Captain Cyril *1/5 Gloucestershire Regiment*	Aug 1916	Thiepval Memorial
Kettle, Lieutenant Thomas *9/Royal Dublin Fusiliers*	Sept 1916	Thiepval Memorial
Tennant, Lieutenant Edward *4/Grenadier Guards*	Sept 1916	Guillemont Military Cem I.B.18
Coulson, Sergeant Leslie *12/London Regiment (The Rangers)*	Oct 1916	Grove Town Cemetery I.J.24
Munro, L/Sergeant Hector (Saki) *22/Royal Fusiliers*	Dec 1916	Thiepval Memorial

Lieutenant William Hodgson.

Captain Cyril Winterbotham.

Lieutenant Gilbert Waterhouse.

Sergeant Hector Munro aka Saki.

Sergeant John Streets.

Second Lieutenant 'Rex' Freston.

FURTHER READING

A veritable library of published titles cover aspects of the Somme – including the first day – and limited space dictates that they cannot all be covered here. Nine of the **Battleground Europe** titles published by **Pen and Sword** – www.pen-and-sword.co.uk – focus on the area covered by this guidebook and provide a host of supplementary information on some of the most visited parts of the area. Here you will find personal experiences of soldiers who served in the area, contemporary photographs and trench maps.

Gommecourt, Nigel Cave
Serre, Jack Horsfall and Nigel Cave
Beaumont-Hamel, Nigel Cave
Thiepval, Michael Stedman
The Germans at Beaumont Hamel, Jack Sheldon
The Germans at Thiepval, Jack Sheldon
La Boisselle, Michael Stedman
Fricourt–Mametz, Michael Stedman
Montauban, Graham Maddocks

Perhaps the seminal work on 1 July 1916 is *The First Day on the Somme* by Martin Middlebrook. First published in 1971, it was one of the first to use oral history – first-hand accounts of the men involved – to tell the story of the fighting. Further personal experiences of first-day survivors are recorded in the many histories of the Pals Battalions that went over the top on 1 July 1916 and which have been published by Pen and Sword, the first of which was that on the *Barnsley Pals* by Jon Cooksey, one of the authors of this guide. Other Pals titles include those on the Accrington, Leeds, Bradford, Salford, Manchester and Liverpool Pals and the Sheffield City Battalion.

There are several published first-hand accounts of those who fought on 1 July 1916 amongst which are such gems as *Tommy at Gommecourt* by Thomas James Higgins. Mary Ellen Freeman's *Poets and Pals of Picardy* from the **Cameos of the Western Front** series is another useful addition to the Somme library, as is the recently updated guide to *Walking the Somme* by Paul Reed. For those battlefield tourists who prefer to tour the Somme battlefronts by car *Major and Mrs Holt's Guide to the Somme* and Rose Coombes' *Before Endeavours Fade* are helpful. A guidebook that covers the wider Somme battlefields in both world wars is *The Middlebrook Guide to the Somme Battlefields* by Martin and Mary Middlebrook, which we have found to be an extremely informative and useful reference along with Gerald Gliddon's updated survey of the Somme battlefields, *Somme 1916*, first published in 1990 as *When the Barrage Lifts*. Three books by Alan Macdonald – *A Lack of Offensive Spirit? – The 46th (North Midland) Division at Gommecourt, 1st July 1916, Pro Patria Mori: The 56th (1st London) Division at Gommecourt, 1st July 1916* and *Z Day, 1st July 1916 – The Attack of the VIII Corps at Beaumont Hamel and Serre* – are amongst volumes that assess the actions of specific units on specific sectors in detail. *Slaughter on the Somme* by Martin Mace and John Grehan is the gathering together – in one volume – of the war diaries of the British battalions that went over the top on the British Army's worst day and is an invaluable reference work.

For battlefield visitors who wish to expand their knowledge in more depth, the following will be of interest:

The Somme, Peter Barton with Jeremy Banning
The Imperial War Museum Book of the Somme, Malcolm Brown
The Somme, Peter Hart
Somme, Lyn Macdonald
Bloody Victory, William Philpott
The Somme, Gary Sheffield

Index

Notes